THE ANCIENT AMERICAN —WORLD—

STUDENT STUDY GUIDE

Oxford University Press, Inc., publishes works that
further Oxford University's objective of excellence
in research, scholarship, and education.

Oxford   New York
Auckland   Cape Town   Dar es Salaam   Hong Kong   Karachi
Kuala Lumpur   Madrid   Melbourne   Mexico City   Nairobi
New Delhi   Shanghai   Taipei   Toronto

With offices in
Argentina   Austria   Brazil   Chile   Czech Republic   France   Greece
Guatemala   Hungary   Italy   Japan   Poland   Portugal   Singapore
South Korea   Switzerland   Thailand   Turkey   Ukraine   Vietnam

Copyright © 2005 by Oxford University Press, Inc.

Published by Oxford University Press, Inc.
198 Madison Avenue, New York, NY 10016
www.oup.com

Oxford is a registered trademark of Oxford University Press

All rights reserved. No part of this publication may be reproduced,
stored in a retrieval system, or transmitted in any form or by any means,
electronic, mechanical, photocopying, recording, or otherwise,
without the prior permission of Oxford University Press.

ISBN-13: 978-0-19-522297-5 (California edition)   ISBN-13: 978-0-19-522163-3

Writer: Susan Moger
Editor: Robert Weisser
Project Editor: Lelia Mander
Project Director: Jacqueline A. Ball
Education Consultant: Diane L. Brooks, Ed.D.
Design: designlabnyc

Casper Grathwohl, Publisher

Printed in the United States of America
on acid-free paper

Dear Parents, Guardians, and Students:

This study guide has been created to increase student enjoyment and understanding of *The Ancient American World*. It has been developed to help students access the text. As they do so, they can learn history and the social sciences and improve reading, language arts, and study skills.

The study guide offers a wide variety of interactive exercises to support every chapter. Parents or other family members can participate in activities labeled "With a Parent or Partner." Adults can help in other ways, too. One important way is to encourage students to create and use a history journal as they work through the exercises in the guide. The journal can simply be an off-the-shelf notebook or three-ring binder used only for this purpose. Some students might like to customize their journals with markers, colored paper, drawings, or computer graphics. No matter what it looks like, a journal is a place a student's very own place to organize thoughts, practice writing, and make notes on important information. It will serve as a personal report of ongoing progress that your child's teacher can evaluate regularly. When completed, it will be a source of satisfaction and accomplishment for your child.

Sincerely,

Casper Grathwohl
Publisher

This book belongs to:

_____

CONTENTS

How to Use the Student Study Guides to *The World in Ancient Times* — 6

Graphic Organizers — 8

Important Vocabulary Words — 10

Chapter 1 — 11
People of Maize: Early Farmers in the Valley of Oaxaca
The people of the ancient American Valley of Oaxaca were efficient and resourceful farmers who lived in small villages and organized the insides of their homes into specific work areas. They believed they were at the mercy of a moody god of rain, and their very existence depended strongly on maize, a type of wild corn.

Chapter 2 — 13
Land of Rubber: The Olmec Civilization
Archaeologists believe that the Olmec civilization was a sister culture of the Valley of Oaxaca and Maya cultures that were growing around the same time. The Olmec lived in the Gulf Coast region of Mexico and are best known for the colossal stone heads they chiseled from volcanic rock.

Chapter 3 — 15
Conquests and Captives: The First Mesoamerican Cities
The great mountaintop city of Monte Albán, built by the Zapotec people, thrived for over 1,000 years. The Maya people built El Mirador in the midst of a swampy jungle, where they very successfully farmed and hunted. The reasons for the decline of these cities are a mystery to archaeologists.

Chapter 4 — 17
Pyramids, Paintings, and Pottery: Teotihuacan, City of the Gods
Archaeologists do not know what group of people built the great city of Teotihuacan, in Central Mexico. It was the location of great contributions to art and religion and is the home of the highest pyramids in Mesoamerica.

Chapter 5 — 19
K'uk' Mo' Takes a Hike: Written History Takes a Leap
Legendary Maya king K'uk' Mo' began a dynasty that lasted for four centuries. Altar Q and other artifacts in Copán, Honduras, tell their dynastic history through carved hieroglyphs and sculptures.

Chapter 6 — 21
The Boy-King of Bone: An Explosion of Maya Hieroglyphs
The kingdom of Bone, now known as Palenque, was a center of Maya art and architecture. The glyphs in its Temple of Inscriptions told a mythical history that elevated Lady Sak K'uk', briefly the ruler of Bone, to the status of goddess and secured political power for her son and grandsons.

Chapter 7 — 23
Fear and Fire: The Fall of Maya Kingdoms
Archaeologists have a variety of theories about why most Maya cities were abandoned by their inhabitants by 800–900 CE. In spite of the decline of the ancient cities, Maya culture continues today.

Chapter 8 — 25
Cotton, Copper, and Canoes: The Rise of the Putún Maya at Chichén Itzá
The Putún Maya were master seafaring traders who took over the Yucatán peninsula and turned the farming city Chichén Itzá into a central site in their trade network of Maya cities.

Chapter 9 — 27
The Feathered Serpent Rides Again: The City of Tula
Legendary Topiltzin Quetzalcoatl was a beloved, godlike figure who may have ruled the Toltec people. The Toltec city of Tula was an artistic and fashionable place that lasted only 200 years.

Chapter 10 — 29
Triple Whammy: Forging the Aztec Empire
The Mexica built the city of Tenochtitlan and struggled to rise from their oppression as servants of Toltec descendants. Mexica king Itzcoatl rose in power and rewrote the history of the Mexica to benefit the nobility so that the common people were completely under his control.

Chapter 11 — 31
Flowers and Song: The Lives of Aztec Families
   Men and women in the Aztec Empire were trained and educated to fulfill very specific societal roles and expectations.

Chapter 12 — 33
War of the Worlds: The Aztec Encounter the Spaniards
   In his quest for gold and control of the Aztec Empire, Spanish conquistador Hernán Cortés and his army brought disease, death, and destruction to Tenochtitlan and the Aztec people.

Chapter 13 — 35
War of the Worlds, Continued: The Inca and the Spaniards in South America
   The Inca Empire, located in the Andes Mountains of South America, was first weakened by internal political struggles and ultimately destroyed by Spanish conquest.

Chapter 14 — 37
Roller-Coaster Roads: Up and Down the Andean World
   Pedro de Cieza de León, a Spaniard, spent 16 years traveling in the Andes Mountains. He wrote a chronicle that described their geography and helped scholars understand the lives of ancient Andeans.

Chapter 15 — 39
A Tale of Two Cities: The Oldest Towns in the Americas
   Archaeologists are excavating and studying the ancient settlements of Aspero and Caral, in Peru, to determine whether they were cities or ceremonial centers.

Chapter 16 — 41
The Thunderous Temple: Andean People Connect
   People came from many different Peruvian cultures to the temple in Chavín de Huántar to make offerings to their supreme god and to ask questions of the oracle. The sacred animal imagery of their ancient religion can be seen in the arts and crafts of the time.

Chapter 17 — 43
On Top of the World: Highland Empires in the Andes
   With a population of as many as 34,000, Tiwanaku, on Lake Titicaca, was the largest city in the ancient Andean world. Four hundred miles to the northeast, farmers in the city of Wari built innovative stone irrigation canals on steep mountain slopes. The ruins of both cities reveal the religious and architectural influence of Chavín.

Chapter 18 — 45
The Man with the Gold Earrings: Moche Artists in Coastal Peru
   Meticulously detailed gold jewelry and sculpted pottery found in pyramids in Sipán, Peru, show that the artists of the Moche kingdom were the finest craftsmen in the ancient Andean world.

Chapter 19 — 47
Chan Chan: Capital City of the Andean Kingdom of Chimor
   The pre-Inca Chimú people built the city of Chan Chan and controlled over 600 miles of coastal Peru until they were conquered and absorbed by the Inca.

Chapter 20 — 49
Cuzco Rules: The Inca in the Land of the Four Quarters
   Like Aztec ruler Itzcoatl, Inca emperor Pachacuti rewrote history and proclaimed himself to be a descendent of the gods. The Inca Empire borrowed many of its traditions from previous cultures.

Chapter 21 — 51
Chosen Girls and Breechcloth Boys: Life in the Inca Empire
   Young Inca children helped their parents with household chores and work in the fields and played games. At age 10 some girls were selected for sacrifice, others to train for specific societal duties. Other girls were expected to marry. Boys celebrated maturity at age 14.

Reports and Special Projects — 54

Library/Media Center Research Log — 55

HOW TO USE THE STUDENT STUDY GUIDES TO
THE WORLD IN ANCIENT TIMES

The World in Ancient Times *will introduce you to some of the greatest civilizations in history, such as ancient Rome, China, and Egypt. You will read about rulers, generals, and politicians. You will learn about scientists, writers, and artists. The daily lives of these people were far different from your life today.*

The study guides to The World in Ancient Times *will help you as you read the books. They will help you learn and enjoy history while building thinking and writing skills. They will also help you pass important tests and just enjoy learning. The sample pages below show the books' special features. Take a look!*

Before you read

- Have a notebook or extra paper and a pen handy to make a history journal. A dictionary and thesaurus will help you too.
- Read the two-part chapter title and predict what you will learn from the chapter.
- Quotation marks in the margin show the sources of ancient writings. The main primary sources are listed next to the chapter title.
- Study all maps and photos. Read the captions closely. (This caption tells that the statue itself is a primary source. Artifacts are records of history, just like writings.)

TOMB, SARCOPHAGUS, AND STATUE FROM ROME; AULUS GELLIUS; AND LIVY

CHAPTER 5
FATHERS, GODS, AND GODDESSES
RELIGION IN ANCIENT ROME

Cornelius Scipio Hispanus was not a modest man. He praised not only himself, but his whole family as well. When he died around 135 BCE, the epitaph written on his tomb listed his many elected offices, followed by four lines of poetry, bragging about his accomplishments:

Tomb from Rome, 135 BCE

> By my good conduct, I heaped honor upon the honor of my family;
> I had children, and I tried to equal the deeds of my father;
> I won the praise of my ancestors and made them glad I was born;
> My own virtue has made noble my family tree.

For generations, the Scipio men had served in high offices. And by the second century BCE, the Scipios had become Rome's leading family. They decorated their family tomb with marble busts of important family members. The oldest sarcophagus contains the body of a Scipio who was a consul of Rome in 298 BCE. Its dedication reads: "Lucius Cornelius Scipio Barbatus, son of Gnaeus, a brave and wise man, whose handsomeness matched his bravery. He was consul, censor, and aedile among you. He captured . . . many cities for Rome and brought home hostages."

Sarcophagus from Rome, 298 BCE

Statue from Rome, 50–25 BCE

Like other patricians, Scipio Hispanus proudly claimed his ancestors as founding fathers of Rome. He was probably much like the Roman in this statue. Even though scholars cannot tell us this person's name, we can learn a lot just by

As you read

- Keep a list of questions.

- Note **boldfaced** words in text. They are defined in the margins. Their *root words* are given in *italics*.

- Look up other unfamiliar words in a dictionary.

- Find important places on the map on pp. 10–11.

- Look up names in Cast of Characters on p. 9 to learn pronunciation.

- Read the sidebars. They contain information to build your understanding.

After you read

- Compare what you have learned with what you thought you would learn before you began the chapter.

FATHERS, GODS, AND GODDESSES | 37

looking at him. First: he's a Roman. We know because he's wearing a toga, the garment that was a sign of manhood. The Romans called it the *toga virilis*, and a boy wasn't allowed to wear it until he became a man, usually at 16. Second, because this unknown Roman is carrying masks of his ancestors, we know that his father or grandfather had served as one of Rome's top officials.

These masks, made of wax or clay, usually hung in the hallways of the ancestral home. Romans took them down and carried them in parades and funeral processions.

Roman families were organized like miniature states, with their own religions and governments. The oldest man in the family was called the **paterfamilias**, the patriarch. He was the boss, and his words were law. Scipio Hispanus was the paterfamilias in his family. This meant that he held lifelong power, even over life and death. He could sell or kill a disobedient slave. He had the right to abandon an unwanted baby, leaving him or her outside to die. Usually this would be a sick child or a baby girl to whom the family couldn't afford to give a dowry when she grew up. Romans wanted healthy sons to carry on the family name, yet a father could imprison, whip, disown, or even execute a son who committed a crime. In 63 BCE, a senator named Aulus Fulvius did exactly that after his son took part in a plot to overthrow the government. But this didn't happen very often. Roman fathers were expected to rule their families with justice and mercy, the same way that political leaders were expected to rule the state.

For both the family and the state, religion played a major role in life. Every Roman home had a shrine to the household gods, the Lares. The father served as the family's priest. Scipio Hispanus would have led his family's prayers and made sacrifices to honor their ancestors and please the gods that protected the entire family—living and dead. When a baby was born, Scipio Hispanus would have hit the threshold of his home with an axe and a broom to frighten away any wild spirits that might try to sneak in. When a household member died, family members carried the body out feet first to make sure that its ghost didn't run back inside. (That's why people still sometimes describe death as "going out feet first.")

> *vir* = "man"
> Roman boys donned the *toga virilis* when they became men. *Virilis* is a form of *vir*; "virile" means "manly."

> *pater* + *familias* = "father" + "family"
> The paterfamilias was the oldest male member of a Roman family.

TOMBS OF THE SCIPIOS

The Romans believed that the dead should neither be buried nor cremated inside the city walls. They were afraid that Rome's sacred places would become polluted by the presence of death. So they lined the roads leading away from Rome with monuments built to house and honor the dead. Visitors can still see the tombs of the Scipios buried along the Appian Way, about two miles from the Forum. (The Appian Way is a military road that was built in the fourth century BCE.)

The next two pages have models of graphic organizers. You will need these to do the activities for each chapter on the pages after that.

Go back to the book as often as you need to.

GRAPHIC ORGANIZERS

As you read and study history, geography, and the social sciences, you'll start to collect a lot of information. Using a graphic organizer is one way to make information clearer and easier to understand. You can choose from different types of organizers, depending on the information.

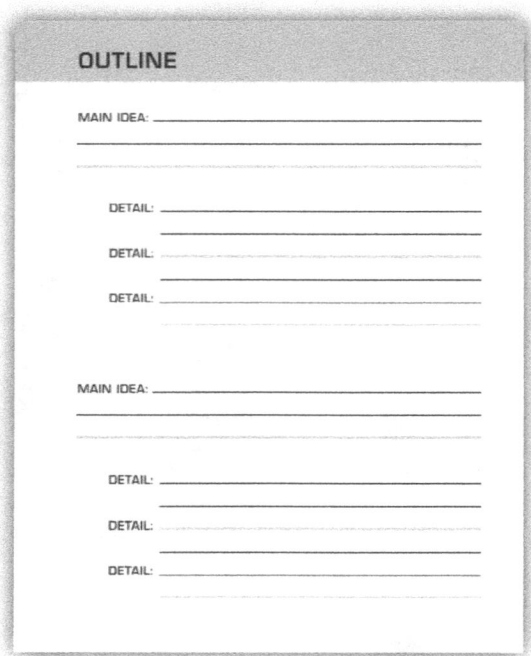

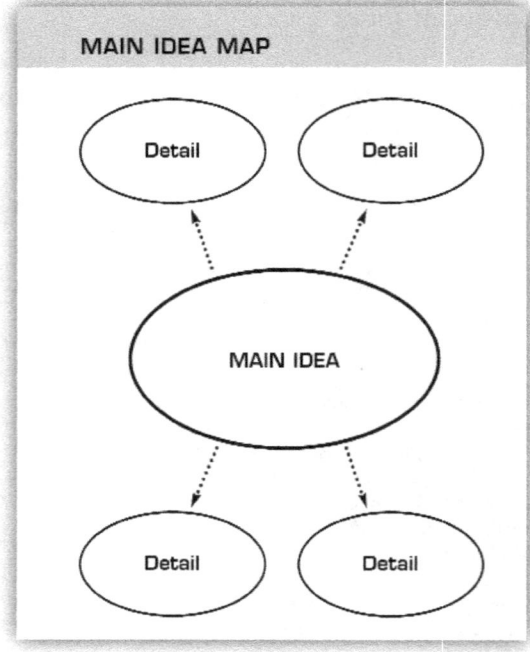

Outline
To build an outline, first identify your main idea. Write this at the top. Then, in the lines below, list the details that support the main idea. Keep adding main ideas and details as you need to.

Main Idea Map
Write down your main idea in the central circle. Write details in the connecting circles.

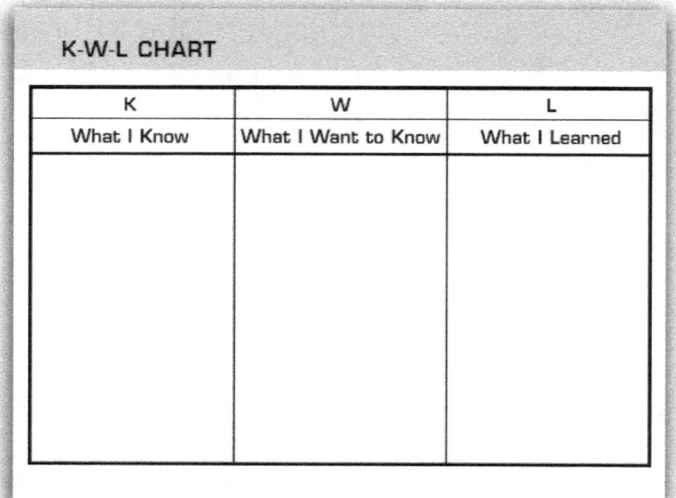

K-W-L Chart
Before you read a chapter, write down what you already know about a subject in the left column. Then write what you want to know in the center column. Then write what you learned in the last column. You can make a two-column version of this. Write what you know in the left and what you learned after reading the chapter.

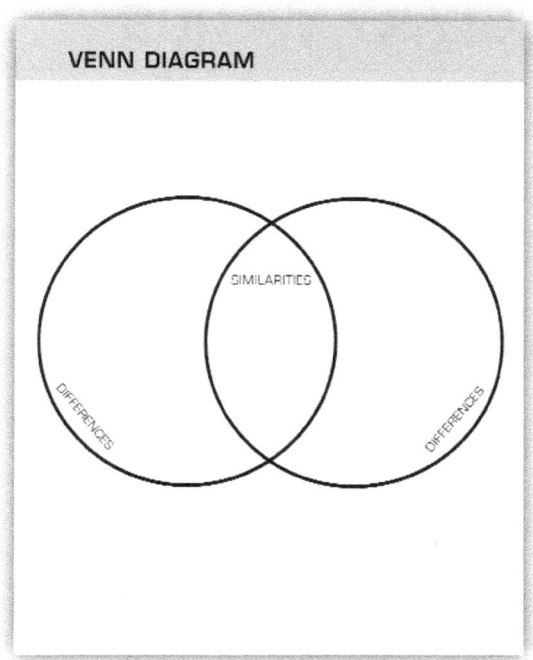

Venn Diagram

These overlapping circles show differences and similarities among topics. Each topic is shown as a circle. Any details the topics have in common go in the areas where those circles overlap. List the differences where the circles do not overlap.

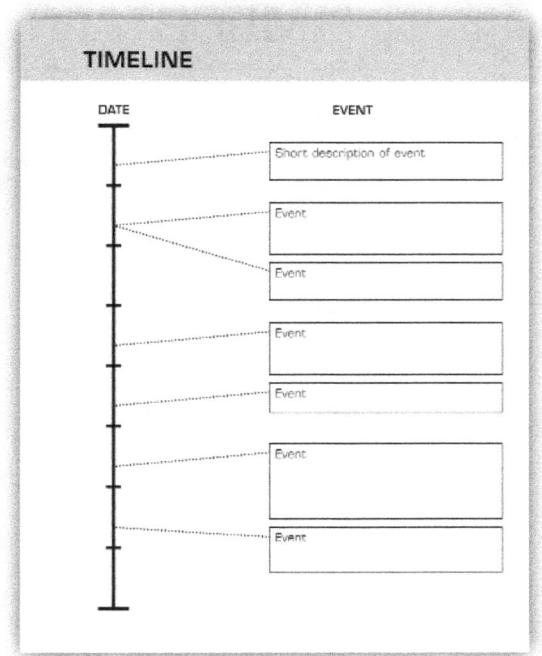

Timeline

A timeline divides a time period into equal chunks of time. Then it shows when events happened during that time. Decide how to divide up the timeline. Then write events in the boxes to the right when they happened. Connect them to the date line.

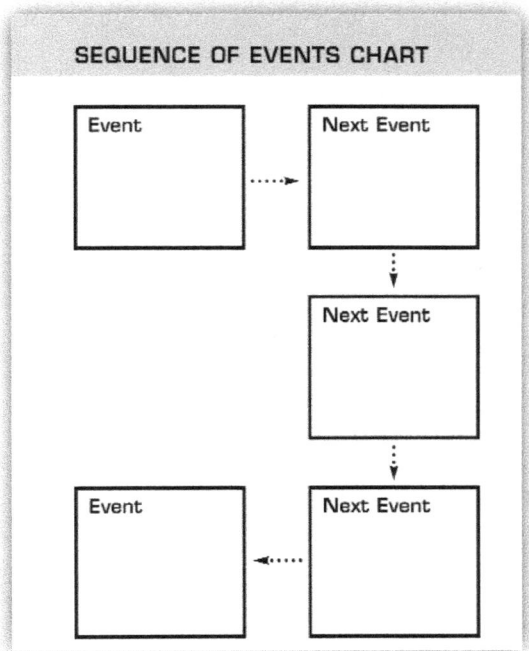

Sequence of Events Chart

Historical events bring about changes. These result in other events and changes. A sequence of events chart uses linked boxes to show how one event leads to another, and then another.

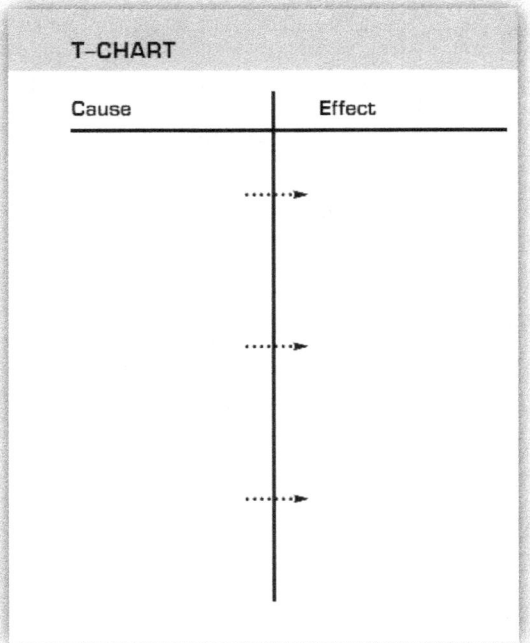

T-Chart

Use this chart to separate information into two columns. To separate causes and effects, list events, or causes, in one column. In the other column, list the change, or effect, each event brought about.

IMPORTANT VOCABULARY WORDS

The Word Bank section of each lesson will give you practive with important vocabulary words from the book. The words below are also important. They're listed in the order in which they appear in each chapter. Use a dictionary to look up any you don't know.

Introduction
nomads
chronicles

Chapter 1
moody
worrisome
shrivel
fickle
vari-colored
spindles
willy-nilly
nutritional
carbohydrates
kernels
tortilla
pot irrigation
terrace
luxury
embroidery
barter

Chapter 2
colossal
basalt
plateau
debris
hearths
mother culture
levees
sacred

Chapter 3
flaunt
codex
sacrificial
sacrifice
barren
irrigation
aggressive
organic
excrement
bumper
canopy
guttural

Chapter 4
refugee
reservoir
deity
majestic
citadel
pandemonium
ceramic
vandal

Chapter 5
table-altar
promotion
reckon
resistance
insignia
dynasty
epigrapher
genealogy

Chapter 6
computation
fateful
prophecy

Chapter 7
chasm
crackle
thatch

Chapter 8
galley
relief
navigate
cenote
architectural

Chapter 9
version
neighborhood
plumage
procession

Chapter 10
persist
upstart
fatal
snub
enclosure
inconvenient
undercover
exploit

Chapter 11
pierce
preparatory
rigorous
essential
inauguration

Chapter 12
ravenous
trek
overwhelm
causeway
abdomen

Chapter 13
gold-plated
virus
incensed
scrape
treacherous
reckless
utmost
consternation
litter
periodically

Chapter 14
whittle
hammock
desolate
hollow
ravine
lugging
quinoa
furrow

Chapter 15
ceremonial
breathtaking
amphitheater
rainforest
potluck

Chapter 16
mucus
oracle
subside
ordeal
supernatural
cult
tie-dyed
solder
renaissance

Chapter 17
splendor
preside
eave
niche

Chapter 18
honeycomb
crumpled
miniature
eyewitness
reenact

Chapter 19
overpower
purveyor
millstone
inheritance
eternity

Chapter 20
successor
showcase
addictive
coincidence
subjugate
hostage
currency
decimal

Chapter 21
sheltered
spindle
dormitory
breechcloth
rebellious
exile
epidemic
quest

CHAPTER 1

PEOPLE OF MAIZE: EARLY FARMERS IN THE VALLEY OF OAXACA

CHAPTER SUMMARY

The people of the ancient American Valley of Oaxaca were efficient and resourceful farmers who lived in small villages and organized the insides of their homes into specific work areas. They believed they were at the mercy of a moody god of rain, and their very existence depended strongly on maize, a type of wild corn.

ACCESS

What kinds of foods do you think the ancient Mesoamericans ate? To help you learn what kinds of plants they grew and animals they hunted, create a main idea map in your history journal similar to the one on page 8 of this study guide. In the large central circle, write *Mesoamerican Foods*. As you read the chapter, in the smaller connecting circles write the types of plant and animal foods that were staples of the farmers of the Oaxaca Valley. You should be able to fill at least 10 connecting circles.

CAST OF CHARACTERS

Answer the following questions in your history journal using complete sentences:

1. Who was the Sky Dragon?
2. On what ancient household item did archaeologists find carvings of the Sky Dragon?

WHAT HAPPENED WHEN?

As you read the chapter, briefly describe what happened on the following dates:

around 5000 BCE _____

16th century CE _____

17th century CE _____

1970s _____

DO THE MATH

How many years passed between 5000 BCE and 1970 CE?

_____

WORD BANK

hypothetical   archaeologist   Maya   hieroglyphics

Fill in the blanks with the correct words from the Word Bank.

1. An _____ studies building ruins, graves, tools, and pottery to learn about ancient history.
2. _____ are signs or symbols that stand for a word, an idea, or a syllable.
3. Almost all _____ books were burned by a Spanish priest.
4. Something that is _____ is a "supposed" or "imagined" idea about how something might have been.

THE ANCIENT AMERICAN WORLD   **11**

WORD PLAY

The chapter tells us that later Mesoamericans wrote *codices*, or handwritten books, about tasks performed by men and women. *Codices* is the plural word for *codex*. In a dictionary, look up *codex* and answer the following questions in your history journal, using complete sentences:

1. What ancient language does *codex* come from?
2. What is the definition of *codex*?

CRITICAL THINKING
COMPARE AND CONTRAST

Mesoamerican women and men had different tasks they had to perform to help their family survive. As you read the chapter you will be able to determine who did which of the tasks listed below. For each task performed by a woman, write "W" on the line next to the task. For each task performed by a man, write "M."

_____ planted maize

_____ ground maize into cornmeal

_____ cooked tortillas

_____ hunted deer

_____ shucked maize kernels from the cobs

_____ spun plant fibers into thread

_____ built houses

_____ harvested maize

_____ wove cloth

_____ made tools from animal bones and obsidian

_____ wove baskets

_____ made clay storage jars

COMPREHENSION

Answer the following questions in your history journal, using complete sentences:

1. What plant foods did the Mesoamericans call the "Three Sisters," and why?
2. How many hours a day did women probably spend grinding maize into cornmeal?
3. What was pot irrigation? Why did the Mesoamericans sometimes have to water their crops this way?

ALL OVER THE MAP

Fill in the map below with the following geographical locations and features:

Gulf of Mexico
Valley of Oaxaca
Rio Balsas
Sierra Madre del Sur
Lake Texcoco
Rio Usumacinta
Gulf of California
Pacific Ocean
Sierra Madre Occidental
Rio Panuco
Rio Grijalva
Caribbean Sea
Rio Papaloapan
Yucatán Peninsula
Sierra Madre Oriental
Valley of Mexico
Rio Santiago-Lerma
Rio Balsas
Rio Grande

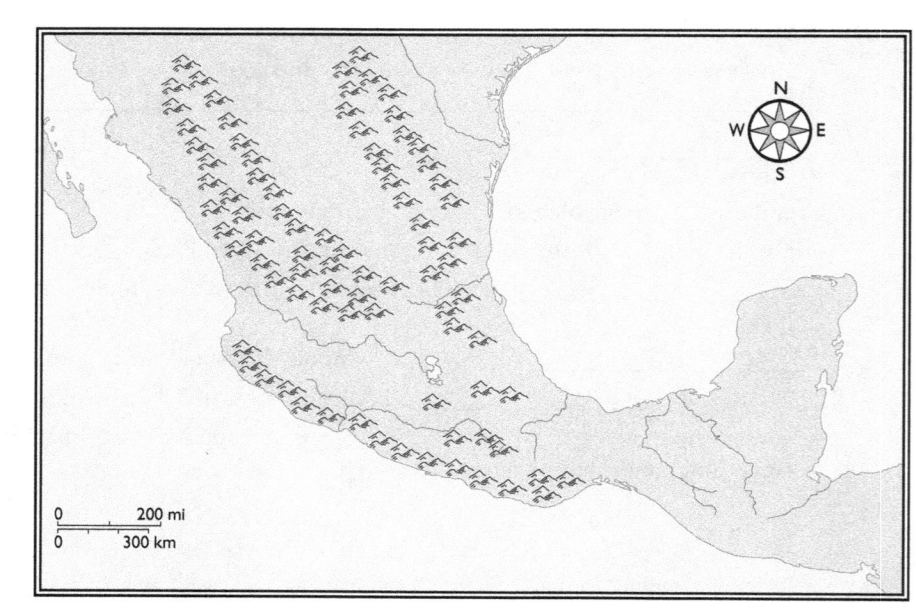

CHAPTER 1

CHAPTER 2
LAND OF RUBBER: THE OLMEC CIVILIZATION

CHAPTER SUMMARY
Archaeologists believe that the Olmec civilization was a sister culture of the Valley of Oaxaca and Maya cultures that were growing around the same time. The Olmecs lived in the Gulf Coast region of Mexico and are best known for the colossal stone heads they chiseled from volcanic rock.

ACCESS
Have you ever heard of the Olmec civilization? What do you know about it? In your history journal, copy the K-W-L graphic organizer on page 8 of this study guide to help you learn more about the culture of the Olmecs and the scientific work done to unearth their secrets. In the *What I Know* column, write what you already know about the Olmec civilization. (If you don't know anything yet, that's okay.) Fill in the *What I Want to Know* column with your questions. As you read the chapter, write the answers to your questions and other interesting facts in the *What I Learned* column.

CAST OF CHARACTERS
Write brief descriptions of the following characters:

Ann Cyphers _____

_____

Matthew and Marion Stirling _____

_____

WHAT HAPPENED WHEN?
Using the timeline graphic organizer on page 9 of this study guide, arrange the following dates from the chapter chronologically from top to bottom on the timeline, then briefly describe what happened during these approximate dates in the corresponding boxes.

1200–600 BCE   as early as 1300 BCE   around 900 BCE   1990–1994 CE

What similar archaeological events happened in the years 1862, 1925, 1940, and 1994?
_____
_____

According to the radiocarbon dating of ancient Olmec wood charcoal, which civilization is older, the Olmec or the Maya? _____

GO FIGURE
Which year came first, 900 CE or 900 BCE? _____

THE ANCIENT AMERICAN WORLD **13**

WORD BANK

Olmec   achiote   Maya   radiocarbon dating   La Venta

Fill in the blanks with the correct words from the Word Bank.

1. _____ is an Olmec settlement 50 miles northeast of the San Lorenzo plateau.
2. Mesoamericans use the _____ root to flavor their chocolate drink.
3. The gigantic basalt heads that the _____ people carved were probably portraits of their leaders.
4. _____ can determine how old a once-living object is by how much of a certain element is still in it.
5. _____ people still live in the eastern third of Mesoamerica.

CRITICAL THINKING
OUTLINE

Archaeologist Ann Cyphers's excavation of the Olmec village of San Lorenzo took time and patience. In your history journal, copy the outline graphic organizer on page 8 of this study guide to help you more fully understand why. Write the main idea of the outline at the top of the page, then fill in several details from the chapter beneath each of the following topics:

Topic I: Why Ann Cyphers wanted to learn about ordinary Olmecs

Topic II: Planning and deciding where to excavate

Topic III: What Cyphers found on the plateau slopes

Topic IV: Evidence of Olmec craft activities

Answer the following questions in your history journal using complete sentences:

1. Where do archaeologists believe the Olmec found the basalt rocks for their colossal sculptures?
2. What two theories explain how the Olmec could have moved the gigantic rocks?

COMPREHENSION

What is a *realm*? Look the word up in your dictionary and write the definition here:
_____
_____

Below are the English names of the gods the ancient Mesoamericans worshipped. Next to each name write the Aztec name of the god and his or her realm.

Warrior Maiden   _____
God of Fire   _____
Smoking Mirror   _____
Wind   _____
God of Hell   _____
Storm God   _____
Sun Disk   _____
Two God   _____
Flower Lord   _____
Young Maize   _____

CHAPTER 3
CONQUESTS AND CAPTIVES: THE FIRST MESOAMERICAN CITIES

CHAPTER SUMMARY
The great mountaintop city of Monte Albán, built by the Zapotec people, thrived for over 1,000 years. The Maya people built El Mirador in the midst of swampy jungle, where they very successfully farmed and hunted. The reasons for the decline of these cities are a mystery to archaeologists.

ACCESS
How did the rulers of ancient Mesoamerican cities maintain their power over thousands of people? Read the description on pages 35–36 of *danzantes*, or conquest slabs, that Monte Albán's leaders had carved and displayed in the city and answer the following questions in your history journal:
1. Who were the people depicted on the conquest slabs in Monte Albán?
2. How were the people clothed and positioned in the pictures on the slabs?
3. What message do you think the leaders of the city tried to send with the pictures on the conquest slabs?
4. Why did the Spanish who saw the conquest slabs in 1519 CE call them *danzantes*?

CAST OF CHARACTERS
What three adjectives can you think of that describe the life or personality of the Zapotec chief One Earthquake? Write them here:

_____

WHAT HAPPENED WHEN?
In your history journal, copy the timeline graphic organizer on page 9 of this study guide. Arrange the following dates from the chapter chronologically from top to bottom on the timeline, then briefly describe what happened on or around these dates in the corresponding boxes.

around 500 BCE   by 400 BCE   about 200 CE   1519 CE
around 900 CE   between 350 and 200 BCE   1926 CE

WORD BANK
stucco   *danzantes*   El Mirador   macaws

Fill in the blanks with the correct words from the Word Bank.
1. Because its jungle location is so difficult to travel to, only eight teams of archaeologists have been to _____ since 1926.
2. _____ are large, brightly colored parrots.
3. The Maya paved the mountaintop with _____, made from burnt limestone powder and water.
4. _____ means "dancers" in Spanish.

WORD PLAY
The chapter tells us that few archaeologists travel to El Mirador because it is so *remote*. The word *remote* has different meanings, depending on whether it is used as a noun or an adjective. Look up both forms of *remote* in a dictionary and write the noun and adjective definitions in your history journal. Then write sentences using each form of the word.

CRITICAL THINKING
CAUSE AND EFFECT

Read the chapter and create a cause and effect graphic organizer in your history journal (see the T-chart on page 9 of this study guide). Below is a list of causes and effects from the chapter that relate to Zapotec life in Monte Albán. Match the causes with their effects in the columns of your graphic organizer.

CAUSE	EFFECT
The three chiefs lived in three arms of land that formed the Oaxaca valley,	SO they controlled enough laborers to build the city.
Archaeologists have found mirrors, shell jewelry, and pottery buried in tombs,	SO a large reservoir was built for storing water.
Together the three chiefs tripled their power,	SO they could unite without giving up their power over their individual lands.
Outside invaders could not attack 20,000 people at once,	SO we know that skilled artists and craftspeople lived in Monte Albán.
Monte Albán had no water supply,	SO they moved to a sacred mountain where they would make their sacrifices.
People wanted to please the rain god with sacrificial blood,	SO city life was safer than country life.

WORKING WITH PRIMARY SOURCES

Stone portrait of One Earthquake's death, San José Mogote, Mexico, 500 BCE

We know a few things about the noble Zapotec warrior from the stone portrait of his death that was displayed at San José Mogote's temple. Read the story of One Earthquake on pages 31–33 and answer the following questions:

1. Why did One Earthquake have a misshapen skull? _____

2. What kinds of things might One Earthquake have done that angered San José Mogote's leader? _____

3. Why do you think the chief of San José Mogote set the slab of One Earthquake's death as a doorsill in his temple? _____

ALL OVER THE MAP

Fill in the map with the cities and geographical features listed below:

El Mirador

Yucatán peninsula

Valley of Oaxaca

Monte Albán

Gulf of Mexico

La Venta

Pacific Ocean

San Lorenzo

San José Mogote

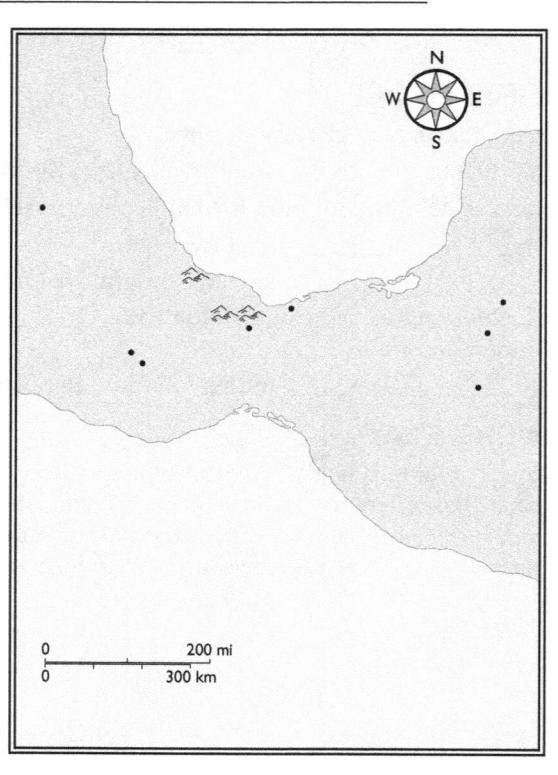

16 CHAPTER 3

CHAPTER 4
PYRAMIDS, PAINTINGS, AND POTTERY: TEOTIHUACAN, CITY OF GODS

CHAPTER SUMMARY

Archaeologists do not know what group of people built the great city of Teotihuacan, in Central Mexico. It was the location of great contributions to art and religion and is the home of the highest pyramids in Mesoamerica.

ACCESS

Archaeologists have developed a theory about why Teotihuacan was built. Read the first two pages of the chapter and answer the following questions in your history journal, using complete sentences:.

1. What natural disasters drove people into the northern part of the Valley of Mexico?

2. List two reasons Fat Mountain might have seemed an ideal spot for a new city.

CAST OF CHARACTERS

According to the chapter, what was unusual about the appearance of the Teotihuacan Storm God?

1. _____

How did warriors in the service of the Storm God imitate his appearance?

2. _____

Where did city builders place the statue of the Goddess of Standing Water?

3. _____

What god is commemorated by ferocious sculptures on the outer walls of the temple called the Citadel?

4. _____

WHAT HAPPENED WHEN?

In your history journal, copy the timeline graphic organizer on page 9 of this study guide. Arrange the following dates from the chapter chronologically from top to bottom on the timeline, then briefly describe what happened during these approximate dates in the corresponding boxes.

50 BCE   400 CE   550 CE

100 CE   600 CE   1960s   1970s

WORD BANK

Teotihuacan   Moon Pyramid

Fill in the blanks with the correct words from the Word Bank.

1. The _____ was built first in the city.

2. _____ is located in central Mexico.

WORD PLAY

Ancient Mesoamericans used *obsidian* to make tools. What is *obsidian*, and where does it come from? Look up *obsidian* in a dictionary and answer those questions in your history journal.

THE ANCIENT AMERICAN WORLD

CRITICAL THINKING

Teotihuacan has some of the most incredible architecture in Mesoamerica. In your history journal, copy the outline graphic organizer on page 8 of this study guide to help you picture some of its landmark structures. Write the main idea of the outline at the top of the page, then fill in several details from the chapter beneath each of the following topics:

Topic I: Moon Pyramid

Topic II: Sun Pyramid

Topic III: The Citadel

Topic IV: The Great Compound

WRITE ABOUT IT

The Aztecs gave the Sun Pyramid its name and told a legend that explained the creation of the sun. Such legends have been created throughout history in different cultures and religions in an attempt to understand the mysterious or unexplainable. To prepare to create your own Mesomerican legend, read the How the Sun Was Born sidebar on page 43. Then read the descriptions of the Storm God on pages 41–42. On a page in your history journal, write a legend that explains the meaning or origin of the mysterious round goggles that the Storm God wears in pictures and why warriors serving him wore them.

ALL OVER THE MAP

Fill in the map with the cities and geographical features listed below.

Valley of Oaxaca

Monte Albán

Teotihuacan

Gulf of Mexico

La Venta

Valley of Mexico

Pacific Ocean

San Lorenzo

San José Mogote

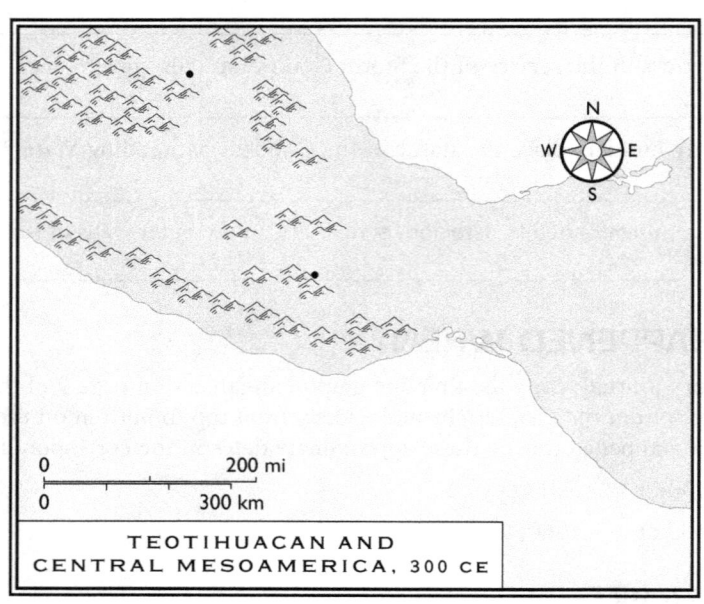

TEOTIHUACAN AND CENTRAL MESOAMERICA, 300 CE

READ MORE

To read more about Teotihuacan and other ancient Mesoamerican cities, see the Further Reading suggestions at the end of *The Ancient American World*.

CHAPTER 5
K'UK' MO' TAKES A HIKE: WRITTEN HISTORY TAKES A LEAP

CHAPTER SUMMARY
Legendary Maya king K'uk' Mo' began a dynasty that lasted for four centuries. Altar Q and other artifacts in Copán, Honduras, tell their dynastic history through carved hieroglyphs and sculptures.

ACCESS
The Maya people in Copán produced more writing than any other Mesoamericans. They used hieroglyphs, which are written or carved signs or pictures that stand for syllables and words. In your history journal, copy the main idea map on page 8 of this study guide to help you understand how hieroglyphs work. In the large central circle, write Types of Glyphs. Read the sidebar about hieroglyphs on page 49 and then in the smaller connecting circles write descriptions of six types of glyphs used by Maya scribes.

CAST OF CHARACTERS
In your history journal, write complete sentences that describe the significance of each of the following people from the chapter.

K'uk' Mo' Ajaw (K'OOK' mo'ah-HOW)   Alfred Maudslay   David Stuart

WHAT HAPPENED WHEN?
426 CE _____

1995 _____

end of 600s CE _____

1884–1886 _____

It took different scholars and archaeologists almost a century to decode the Altar Q hieroglyphs, little by little. Create a mini-timeline in your history journal using the following dates, and briefly describe how progress was made over the years toward understanding the identity of K'uk' Mo'.

1912   1970s   1980s   1985

WORD BANK
Altar Q   stela   epigraphers   Popol Vuh

Fill in the blanks with the correct words from the Word Bank. One word is not used.

1. _____ study ancient inscriptions written on stone, pottery, and other artifacts.

2. The _____, written by the Maya, is a family history that describes how the gods created the world.

3. _____ tells the story of the kings of Copán in hieroglyphs.

THE ANCIENT AMERICAN WORLD

WORD PLAY

What is an *altar*? Look the word up in a dictionary, and answer the following questions in your history journal:

1. What are some of the languages the word *altar* may come from?
2. How have people sometimes used *altars*?

Look up in a dictionary the extra word from the Word Bank. Write a sentence using that word.

___

COMPREHENSION
SEQUENCE OF EVENTS

We know some of the history of K'uk' Mo' from translations of the 2,200 glyphs on the Hieroglyphic Stairway in Copán. Read the translated story of K'uk' Mo' on pages 47–50 of the chapter. Then copy the sequence of events graphic organizer in your history journal (see page 9 of this study guide). Organize the following events from the story in the correct order.

- Three days went by, and the name of K'uk' Mo' Ajaw was changed to K'inich Yax K'uk' Mo', to represent his promotion from lord to great sun.
- K'uk' Mo' found a wife, and they had a son.
- It took five months for K'uk' Mo' to walk from Teotihuacan to "three mountain place" (Copán).
- K'uk' Mo' went to a special location, probably in Teotihuacan, to undergo a ritual to become a king.
- K'uk' Mo' was given special goggles to wear, made out of cut shell, and a shield decorated with the image of the War Serpent God.
- K'uk' Mo' left the city of the gods for the trip home—a difficult journey over rough and dangerous terrain.

1. What are the English translations of the names K'uk' Mo' Ajaw and K'inich Yax K'uk' Mo'?

   _____

   _____

2. What was the name of the son of K'uk' Mo'? _____

3. K'uk' Mo' wore or carried special items that represented certain gods. What three gods does the chapter tell us K'uk' Mo' honored in his manner of dress?

   _____

WORKING WITH PRIMARY SOURCES

Inscription on top of Altar Q, Copán (763 CE)

Epigrapher David Stuart figured out that the headdress of the mystery figure on Altar Q, with its drawings of a quetzal feather, a macaw head, and the glyphs for "sun" and "green," represented the four parts of the name K'inich Yax K'uk' Mo'. What if, rather than using an alphabet, we wrote in pictures and glyphs today? Give it a try. On a page in your history journal, write your full name. Then beneath your name, create a series of pictures and symbols that are meaningful to you, to represent the different parts of your name. You can create a symbol or picture for each syllable, or for your first, middle, and last names.

CHAPTER 6

THE BOY-KING OF BONE: AN EXPLOSION OF MAYA HIEROGLYPHS

CHAPTER SUMMARY

The kingdom of Bone, now known as Palenque, was a center of Maya art and architecture. The glyphs in its Temple of Inscriptions told a mythical history that elevated Lady Sak K'uk', briefly the ruler of Bone, to the status of goddess and secured political power for her son and grandsons.

ACCESS

The chapter tells us that Lady Sak K'uk' ruled the kingdom of Bone for a brief three years and that those years were probably a time of sorrow and chaos. After you read the first two pages of the chapter, answer the following questions in your history journal using complete sentences:

1. Why was it disastrous that Lady Sak K'uk's father, the king of Bone, died without naming a successor?
2. Do scholars know how Lady Sak K'uk' became ruler of Bone?
3. What are some scholars' ideas about why Lady Sak K'uk's reign may have been a time of great chaos?

CAST OF CHARACTERS

In your history journal, write a brief description of each of the following from the chapter:

Scroll Serpent   Lady Sak K'uk' (SAHK kuh-OOK)   K'inich Janaab' Pakal I

What were the names of the 16th-century Spaniards who wrote about the education of Maya and Aztec children at the time of the Spanish conquest?

___

WHAT HAPPENED WHEN?

In your history journal, copy the timeline graphic organizer on page 9 of this study guide. Arrange the following dates from the chapter chronologically from top to bottom on the timeline, then briefly describe what happened during these approximate dates in the corresponding boxes:

599 CE   611 CE   612 CE   647 CE   673 CE
July 29, 615 CE   1956   1990

WORD BANK

sarcophagus   mosaic   self-appointed   fateful

Complete the sentences below with the correct words from the Word Bank. One word is not used.

1. Lady Sak K'uk' was the _____ ruler of Bone for three years.
2. The burial chamber of K'inich Janaab' Pakal I contained a stone _____ for his body.
3. Pakal's _____ burial mask was made of pieces of jade.

WORD PLAY

What is a *deity*? What does it mean to *deify* someone? Look up both words in your dictionary and write their definitions in your history journal. Then answer the following questions:

1. What is the Latin word that *deity* comes from?
2. What word with the same root, *dei*, means "the act of killing a divine being"?

CRITICAL THINKING

Pakal built the Temple of Inscriptions to strengthen the idea that his mother, Lady Sak K'uk', was the goddess First Mother and to provide a burial place for himself. Use the outline graphic organizer on page 8 of this study guide to help in understanding the design of the Temple of Inscriptions. Write the main idea of the outline at the top of the page, then fill in several details from the chapter beneath each of the following topics:

Topic I: The location of the Temple of Inscriptions

Topic II: Pakal's burial chamber

Topic III: How the glyphs inscribed in the temple reinforced the idea of Lady Sak K'uk' as goddess

COMPREHENSION

Circle the correct answers.

1. What is the Maya word for *Bone*?
    a. Palenque
    b. B'aakal
    c. Pakal

2. Why couldn't Lady Sak K'uk's husband rule Bone?
    a. He wasn't brave.
    b. He wasn't noble.
    c. He wasn't descended from a royal family.

3. At his crowning, Pakal wore water lilies in his hair to signify that
    a. under his rule, lots of flowers would grow.
    b. the city he governed would flow with rivers and streams.
    c. he wanted everyone to wear flowers in their hair.

4. The First Mother was the goddess of
    a. creation.
    b. water.
    c. the moon.

5. Pakal lived to the age of
    a. 12.
    b. 44.
    c. 81.

CHAPTER 7

FEAR AND FIRE: THE FALL OF MAYA KINGDOMS

CHAPTER SUMMARY

Archaeologists have a variety of theories about why most Maya cities were abandoned by their inhabitants by 800–900 CE. In spite of the decline of the ancient cities, Maya culture continues today.

ACCESS

What kinds of things do you think the Maya people left behind when they abandoned their beautiful cities? To explore the subject, in your history journal create a main idea map graphic organizer similar to the one on page 8 of this study guide. In one large central circle, write *What the Maya Left Behind*. Then, as you read the chapter, in smaller connecting circles write several of the types of artifacts archaeologists have discovered.

CAST OF CHARACTERS

Briefly describe the following people from the chapter:

Bol (BOWL) _____

Takeshi Inomata _____

Rebecca Storey _____

WHAT HAPPENED WHEN?

early 800s CE _____

800–900 CE _____

1993 _____

WORD BANK

anemia   flourish   clamber   alliance

Complete the sentences below with the correct words from the Word Bank. One word is not used.

1. _____ is a medical condition than causes fatigue.

2. Cities that join forces to fight a more powerful city form an _____.

3. In order to destroy the city of Aguateca, warriors had to _____ over its walls.

WORD PLAY

Team up with a classmate to figure out the meaning of *anthropology*. The word has two parts: *anthropo-* and *-logy*. In your dictionaries, one of you should look up *anthropo*, and the other can look up *logy*. Put together the meanings, and then in your history journals, write down the definition and a complete sentence using the word *anthropology*.

THE ANCIENT AMERICAN WORLD

CRITICAL THINKING
FACT OR OPINION?

A fact is a statement that can be proved. An opinion is a statement that can be neither proved nor disproved. Read the chapter, and for each statement about the fall and excavation of the Maya city of Aguateca below write "F" or "O" to indicate whether it is a fact or an opinion.

_____ Since 1993, archaeologists have been studying the ruins of Aguateca.

_____ It is likely that the royal family had already escaped.

_____ The warriors must have been furious to find the palace deserted.

_____ Takeshi Inomata excavated the home of Bol the Scribe.

_____ If the invasion began at night, perhaps Bol was asleep.

_____ Inomata found a seashell ornament carved with Bol's name and title.

_____ Bol may have removed the ornament before falling asleep.

_____ We don't know what happened to Bol.

Briefly describe what invaders hoped to accomplish by destroying the palace at Aguateca.

_____

COMPREHENSION
SUMMARIZING

Archaeologists believe there were several possible reasons the Maya would have deserted their cities. To help you understand these reasons, create six large boxes on a page in your history journal. At the top of each box, write one of the following titles:

Drought

Erosion

Disease/Illness

Interrupted Trade

War Alliances with Other Cities

As you read the chapter, in each box write a few details about how each reason could have caused or contributed to the abandonment of the Maya cities.

Answer the following questions in your history journal using complete sentences:

1. How many Maya are there in the world today?
2. How many Mayan languages are now spoken?
3. What are two Maya traditions that have survived since ancient times?

GROUP TOGETHER

Wouldn't it be interesting to talk with other students about why the Maya people abandoned their cities? Which theories seem the most plausible? Get a few friends together and ask your teacher to help you organize a discussion group at school. Have one person take notes and another person present the group's ideas to the class.

24 CHAPTER 7

CHAPTER 8
COTTON, COPPER, AND CANOES: THE RISE OF THE PUTÚN MAYA AT CHICHÉN ITZÁ

CHAPTER SUMMARY
The Putún Maya were master seafaring traders who took over the Yucatán Peninsula and turned the farming city of Chichén Itzá into a central site in their trade network of Maya cities.

ACCESS
Have you ever heard of Chichén Itzá and its magnificent pyramid? Use the K-W-L graphic organizer on page 8 of this study guide to help you learn more about Chichén Itzá and its evolution from farming community to center of Mesoamerican commerce. In the *What I Know* column, write what you already know about Chichén Itzá. (If you don't know anything yet, that's okay.) Fill in the *What I Want to Know* column with your questions. As you read the chapter, write the answers to your questions and other interesting facts in the *What I Learned* column.

CAST OF CHARACTERS
Briefly describe the following people from the chapter:

Christopher Columbus _____

Bartholomew Columbus _____

Ferdinand Columbus _____

WHAT HAPPENED WHEN?
1502 _____

918 CE _____

500 BCE _____

WORD BANK
awnings   mantles   intricate   efficient

Complete the sentences below with the correct words from the Word Bank. One word is not used.

1. The Maya trading canoes used _____ to provide protection from the rain and waves.
2. Among the goods in the canoes were hatchets made of copper, wine made of maize, and _____, or cloaks, made of cotton.
3. The carvings found in the Temple of the Warriors are _____, with many details.

CRITICAL THINKING
COMPARE AND CONTRAST
The Putún Maya were very different in many ways from the Yucatán Maya. To explore their differences and similarities, create a Venn diagram in your history journal with two circles, similar to the graphic organizer on page 9 of this study guide. In one circle write *Putún Maya*, and in the other write *Yucatán Maya*. As you read the chapter, write the details listed below about each group in the appropriate circle. Any characteristics shared by the two groups should be written in the space where the circles overlap.

THE ANCIENT AMERICAN WORLD

- Wore shoulder capes
- Captain Sun Disk
- Had long hair with short bangs
- In battle, carried round shields painted with dots
- Hauled trade goods slowly overland on people's backs
- Worshipped the Feathered Serpent god
- Spoke Mayan

- Were farmers
- Hauled trade goods by canoe
- Resisted the takeover of Chichén Itzá
- In battle, carried rectangular shields
- Captain Serpent
- Worshipped the rain god, Chac
- Were expert watermen and traders
- Won the battle for control of Chichén Itzá

COMPREHENSION

SEQUENCE OF EVENTS

As you read the description on pages 68–69 of typical Putún trade journey, use the sequence of events graphic organizer on page 9 of this study guide to organize the events below in correct order from first to last.

- The trader sails up the west coast of the Yucatán peninsula with the bowls.
- In Cozumel, the trader barters his salt for spiny oyster shells from the Pacific Ocean.
- A Putún trader in Tabasco exchanges cacao pods for a shipment of bowls.
- The bowls are traded for a pile of embroidered cloaks.
- The trader heads back home to Tabasco with the oyster shells to begin the circle of trade again.
- The trader and his crew head to Isla Cerritos, where the merchant trades the cloaks for blocks of salt.
- Hired porters and slaves haul the bowls inland to Chichén Itzá.

ALL OVER THE MAP

On the map, label the locations and geographical features listed below.

- Isla Cerritos
- Cozumel
- Gulf of Honduras
- Tabasco
- Yucatán Peninsula
- Chichén Itzá
- Highlands
- Gulf of Mexico
- Rio Usumacinta
- Caribbean Sea

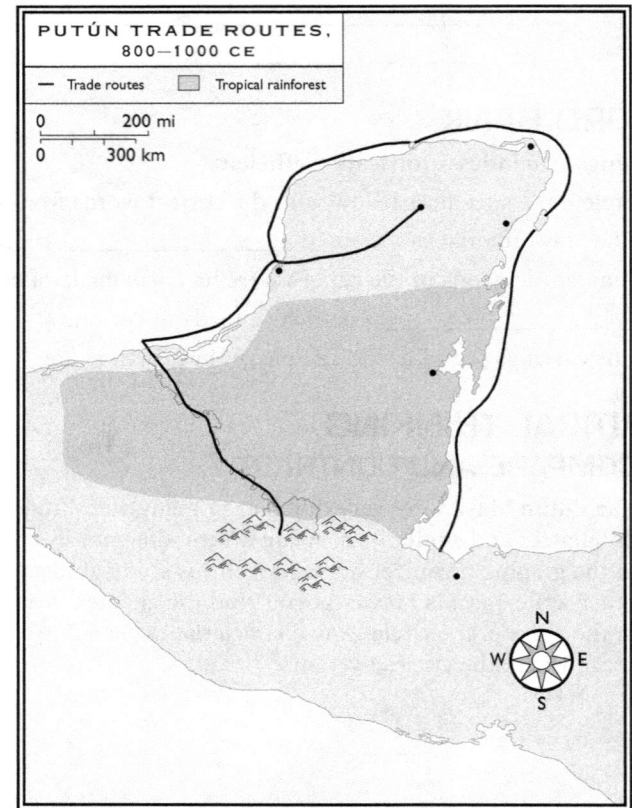

26 CHAPTER 8

CHAPTER 9

THE FEATHERED SERPENT RIDES AGAIN: THE CITY OF TULA

CHAPTER SUMMARY

Legendary Topiltzin Quetzalcoatl was a beloved, godlike figure who may have ruled the Toltec people. The Toltec city of Tula was an artistic and fashionable place that lasted only 200 years.

ACCESS

Who might Topiltzin Quetzalcoatl actually have been? How was he depicted in Toltec art? Was he a real man? Who did the Toltecs say he was? To explore these questions, create a main idea map graphic organizer in your history journal similar to the one on page 8. In the large central circle, write *TQ*. As you read the first two pages of the chapter, in the smaller connecting circles write several facts that answer your questions about Topiltzin Quetzalcoatl.

CAST OF CHARACTERS

Who collected all the information about ancient Mesoamerica that is found in the *Florentine Codex*?

_____

What nickname did archaeologists give to Topiltzin Quetzalcoatl?

_____

WHAT HAPPENED WHEN?

Using the timeline graphic organizer on page 9, arrange the following dates from the chapter chronologically from top to bottom on the timeline, then briefly describe what happened during these approximate dates in the corresponding boxes.

| 16th century CE | between 700–900 CE | 1519 CE | around 1588 |
| by 950 CE | shortly before 900 CE | | |

What happened to the city of Tula by 1150 CE? _____

WORD BANK

paradise   wily   monumental   penance

Complete the sentences below with the correct words from the Word Bank. One word is not used.

1. When Topiltzin Quetzalcoatl thought he had offended the gods, he did _____ to apologize.

2. In the words of the storytellers, Tula became a heavenly place, or a _____.

3. Many of Tula's public buildings were huge, or _____.

WORD PLAY

A passage from the *Florentine Codex* says that Topiltzin Quetzalcoatl was "summoned by the sun." What does it mean to *summon* someone? Look the word up in a dictionary, then in your history journal write sentences that use the words *summon* and *summoned*.

CRITICAL THINKING

OUTLINE

Tula was a civilized and comfortable place to live that attained legendary status in the centuries after its destruction. Use the outline graphic organizer on page 8 of this study guide to understand what legends say happened to Tula. Write the main idea of the outline at the top of the page, and then fill in several details from the chapter beneath each of the following topics.

Topic I: The art of Tula

Topic II: The legend of heavenly Tula

Topic III: The evil priests and their puppet show

Topic IV: TQ's revenge and grief

Topic V: The loyalty of Tula's people

COMPARE AND CONTRAST

The cities of Tula and Teotihuacan are similar in many ways. Explore this idea by creating a Venn diagram in your history journal with two circles, similar to the graphic organizer on page 9 of this study guide. In one circle write *Tula*, and in the other write *Teotihuacan*. As you read the chapter, write the details listed below about each city in the appropriate circles. Any characteristics the cities shared get written in the space where the circles overlap.

- Enemies partly burned it around 600 CE
- Has two pyramids
- Enemies burned it around 900 CE
- Beautiful art and architecture
- Has apartment compounds
- Warriors in art wear the goggles of the Storm God
- Ended in 900 CE
- Ended around 1150 CE

Answer the following questions, using complete sentences:

1. What names do archaeologists use for the old city of Tula and the rebuilt part of Tula?

   _____
   _____
   _____

2. How did descendants of the Toltecs feel about themselves and their ancestors?

   _____
   _____
   _____

CHAPTER 10
TRIPLE WHAMMY: FORAGING THE AZTEC EMPIRE

CHAPTER SUMMARY

The Mexica built the city of Tenochtitlan and struggled to rise from their oppression as servants of Toltec descendants. Mexica king Itzcoatl rose in power and rewrote the history of the Mexica to benefit the nobility so that the common people were completely under his control.

CAST OF CHARACTERS

The dramatic story of the birth of the Aztec Empire boasts some colorful characters, both mythical and real. As you read the chapter, write three facts about each of the following characters in your history journal:

Fray Diego Durán   Mexi   Itzcoatl (EETZ-ko-aht)   Serpent Woman

WHAT HAPPENED WHEN?

about 1000 CE _____

by 1367 CE _____

1428 CE _____

1521 CE _____

1581 CE _____

WORD BANK

multiple   vassals   spoils   tribute

Complete the sentences below with the correct words from the Word Bank. One word is not used.

1. The Mexica became _____, or servants, of the Tepanec people.

2. Commoners in the Aztec kingdom rebelled against the tax system that forced them to pay more _____ to the king.

3. Because nobles were allowed to have _____ wives, they often had many children.

WORD PLAY

Find the word *lackeys* in the chapter on page 79. In the context of the sentence in the chapter, what do you think the word *lackeys* means? In your history journal, write a sentence that explains your understanding of the word. Then look up *lackey* in a dictionary and write down the definition.

THE ANCIENT AMERICAN WORLD   **29**

CRITICAL THINKING
CAUSE AND EFFECT

Read the chapter and create a cause and effect graphic organizer in your history journal (see the T-chart on page 9 of this study guide). Below is a list of causes and effects from the chapter that relate to the false version of Mexica history created by Itzcoatl and his nephew, Serpent Woman. Match the causes with their effects in the columns of your graphic organizer.

CAUSE	EFFECT
Children of commoners were not taught the new history in school,	SO thousands of commoners were sacrificed to the god of the sun.
Only nobles could wear shoes and cotton clothing,	SO he and Serpent Woman wrote a history that explained why only the king and royal families should be wealthy.
Serpent Woman created a new national religion that required massive human sacrifice,	SO if any of them grew up and became priests and told the old history, the king labeled them evil carriers of false wisdom.
Itzcoatl worried that he and the nobility would have to share their wealth with the non-royal Mexica,	SO any commoner who dared to dress well or even wear jewelry was put to death.

MAKING INFERENCES

Itzcoatl and Serpent Woman created a false history about the Mexica, in which cowardly commoners promised to forever serve and pay tribute to the brave nobility. On page 82, the chapter tells us, "It was all lies, of course, but writing them down made them seem true." Answer the following questions in your history journal, using complete sentences:

1. Why do you think writing down lies as history could make them seem true or make people believe them?
2. What is *propaganda*? Write what you think the word means, then look *propaganda* up in a dictionary and write down the definition.

ALL OVER THE MAP

Write in the locations and geographical features listed below on the map.

- Tula
- Tenochtitlan
- Lake Texcoco
- Tlacopan
- Texcoco

READ MORE

To read more about the Aztec Empire, see the Further Reading suggestions at the end of *The Ancient American World*.

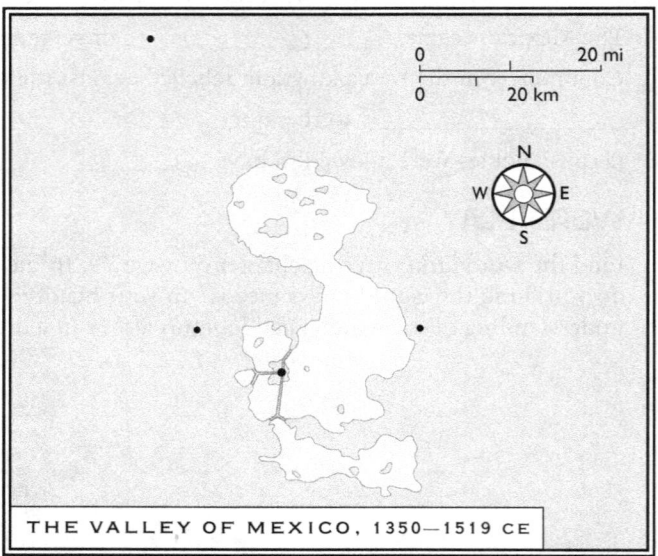

THE VALLEY OF MEXICO, 1350—1519 CE

CHAPTER 11
FLOWERS AND SONG: THE LIVES OF AZTEC FAMILIES

CHAPTER SUMMARY

Men and women in the Aztec Empire were trained and educated to fulfill very specific societal roles and expectations.

ACCESS

How do you think the lives of Aztec men and women differed? Use the K-W-L graphic organizer on page 8 to help you learn more about what was expected of them by their culture. In the *What I Know* column, write what you already know or suspect about the lives of Aztec women and men. (If you don't know anything yet, that's okay.) Fill in the *What I Want to Know* column with your questions. As you read the chapter, write the answers to your questions and other interesting facts in the *What I Learned* column.

CAST OF CHARACTERS

In your history journal, write a complete sentence describing each of these characters:

Fray Bernardino de Sahagún   Moctezuma II (Moke-teh-ZOO-mah)

WHAT HAPPENED WHEN?

Briefly describe what happened on these dates:

1502 CE _____

1521 CE _____

WORD BANK

humiliation   essential   gala   forbidden

Complete the sentences below with the correct words from the Word Bank. One word is not used.

1. To celebrate the inauguration of Moctezuma II, the city of Tenochtilan held a great party, or _____.

2. It would be an embarrassment, or _____, for an Aztec warrior to capture anyone of lower rank.

3. Bad manners were _____ for Aztec children.

WORD PLAY

Many Aztec boys were sent to a strict school that was like a *seminary*. Do you know what a *seminary* is? Look the word up in a dictionary and write its definition in your history journal. Then use *seminary* in a complete sentence.

THE ANCIENT AMERICAN WORLD

CRITICAL THINKING
COMPARE AND CONTRAST

Aztec women and men had different expectations in Aztec culture. As you read the chapter you will be able to determine which of the tasks and descriptions listed below applied to men, and which to women. On the line next to each item, write "W" for "woman," "M" for "man," or "B" if it applies to both.

_____ kept their mother's last name	_____ warrior in the emperor's army
_____ worked in the *chinampas*	_____ dedicated at the temple as an infant
_____ cooked _____ gardened	_____ had pierced ears
_____ wove cloth for trading	_____ was a stone worker
_____ was a blacksmith	_____ was considered a brave warrior for giving birth
_____ in battles, had to capture someone of their own rank or higher	
_____ was taught weaving and spinning	_____ could inherit land and property

OUTLINE

Aztec boys went to schools that trained them to follow specific paths in life. Use the outline graphic organizer on page 8 of this study guide to gain understanding of the types of education boys might have received. Write the main idea of the outline at the top of the page, and then fill in several details from the chapter beneath each of the following topics:

Topic I: Warrior School

Topic II: House of Song

Topic III: School for priests and government workers

WRITE ABOUT IT

At 15, a young Aztec noblewoman would undergo training to become a priestess who cared for the temple and, by age 18, helped direct festivals and ceremonies. Imagine that you are a young Aztec woman who in the morning fulfills her temple duties and later in the day assists in a feast for the Mother Goddess. On a page in your history journal, write a diary entry that describes your day. Be creative, and express your feelings about your life and tasks.

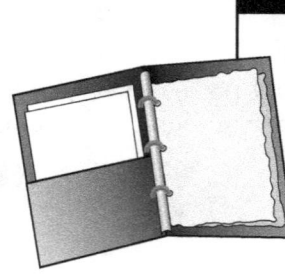

HISTORY JOURNAL

Don't forget to share your history journal with your classmates, and ask if you can see what their journals look like. You might be surprised—and get some new ideas.

CHAPTER 12
WAR OF THE WORLDS: THE AZTEC ENCOUNTER THE SPANIARDS

CHAPTER SUMMARY

In a quest for gold and control of the Aztec Empire, Spanish conquistador Hernán Cortés and his army brought disease, death, and destruction to Tenochtitlan and the Aztec people.

ACCESS

As you read the first pages of the chapter, answer the following questions in your history journal, using complete sentences:

1. How many soldiers did Hernán Cortés bring with him from Spain to Aztec territory?
2. What weapons did the Spanish soldiers carry?
3. How many native warriors and enslaved native women traveled with the army?

CAST OF CHARACTERS

Briefly describe the significance of each of the following characters.

Hernán Cortés (err-NAHN cor-TESS) _____

Bernal Díaz (bear-NAHL DEE-ahz) _____

Malintzin (mahl-EEN-tzeen) _____

Moctezuma II (Moke-teh-ZOO-mah)_____

WHAT HAPPENED WHEN?

Using the timeline graphic organizer on page 9 of this study guide, arrange the following dates from the chapter chronologically from top to bottom on the timeline, then briefly describe what happened during these approximate dates in the corresponding boxes.

November 6, 1519 CE   November 8, 1519 CE   June 30, 1520 CE

August 1521 CE   1584 CE

WORD BANK

ravenous   adobe   vaccine   mestizo

Complete the sentences below with the correct words from the Word Bank. One word is not used.

1. Many Aztecs died of smallpox because they had no _____ to prevent it.
2. Malintzin's mixed-blood son was among the first _____ children born in the Americas.
3. _____ was a popular building material in Tenochtitlan.

WORD PLAY

The Aztec people had no *immunity* to the diseases the Spaniards brought with them from Europe. What is *immunity*? Look the word up in a dictionary and write down the definition in your history journal. Then use *immunity* in a complete sentence.

THE ANCIENT AMERICAN WORLD

COMPREHENSION
SEQUENCE OF EVENTS

From the time that Cortés and his army entered Tenochtitlan, or perhaps before, the Aztec Empire was doomed. As you read in the chapter the description on pages 91–96 of the interactions between Cortés and Moctezuma, use the sequence of events graphic organizer on page 9 of this study guide to organize the events below in correct order from first to last.

- Cortés insisted that Moctezuma turn over his entire fortune as tribute to the Spanish king.
- Cortés tricked Moctezuma with words and took him prisoner.
- Just in case Cortés was the god Topiltzin Quetzalcoatl, Moctezuma gave the Spaniards a warm welcome.
- Native people attacked the fleeing Spaniards at night, killing one third of the Spanish army.
- As a prisoner, Moctezuma was treated politely and allowed to have his usual comforts.
- The Spaniards fled the city with all the gold they could carry.
- Moctezuma was killed, either by Spaniards stabbing him, or by angry warriors throwing stones at him.

Answer the following questions:

1. When Cortés and his men returned to Tenochtitlan, what actions did they take to finally and completely destroy the city and its people?
   _____

2. What diseases brought by the Spanish soldiers killed about 90 percent of the native population within 100 years? _____

THINK ABOUT IT

After you read the chapter, answer the following questions about the slave girl Malintzin, Cortés's translator, in your history journal, using complete sentences:

1. How did Malintzin originally become a slave?
2. How did Malintzin become a translator for Cortés?
3. What did Malintzin hope might happen if she did her job well?
4. How did Malintzin help Cortés enter the city of Tenochtitlan?

WITH A PARENT OR PARTNER

The chapter tells us that after the Spanish conquest, Native Americans saw Malintzin as a traitor who had helped the enemy, but many people now see Malintzin as a woman who used her intelligence to survive slavery. Which side do you agree with? Discuss the following questions with a parent or partner. Take notes on your conversation in your history journal.

1. What do you think Malintzin's life as a slave was like?
2. Do you think Malintzin had a choice about whether or not to learn to translate for Cortés?
3. What do you think you would have done if you were living in Malintzin's circumstances?

CHAPTER 13
WAR OF THE WORLDS, CONTINUED: THE INCA AND THE SPANIARDS IN SOUTH AMERICA

CHAPTER SUMMARY

The Inca Empire, located in the Andes Mountains of South America, was first weakened by internal political struggles and ultimately destroyed by Spanish conquest.

CAST OF CHARACTERS

A variety of characters, both Inca and Spanish, played parts in the weakening and destruction of the Inca Empire. As you read the chapter, write a brief description of each of the following characters in your history journal:

Huayna Capac (WHY-nah KAH-pahk)

Guamán Poma (gwa-MAHN PO-mah)

Francisco Pizarro (fran-CEES-co pee-SAHR-ro)

Pedro de Cieza de León (PEH-dro deh see-EH-sah deh leh-OAN)

Atahualpa (ah-tah-WHAL-pa)

Huascar Inca

Hernando De Soto

Manco Capac

WHAT HAPPENED WHEN?

1493 _____

1567–1615 _____

November 15, 1532 _____

1552 _____

WORD BANK

petite   scrape   blunder   ascent

Complete the sentences below with the correct words from the Word Bank. One word is not used.

1. To reach Cajamarca, Pizarro and his men had to make a difficult _____ into the Andes.

2. The llamas that carried loads for the Inca were _____ in comparison to the Spaniards' huge horses.

3. Atahualpa made a dreadful _____: none of his men was armed.

WORD PLAY

Huayna Capac never named a *successor*, so after his death civil war erupted in the Inca Empire. Knowing this, what do you think the word *successor* means? In your history journal, write a sentence that explains your understanding of the word. Then look up the words *succeed*, *succession*, and *successor* in a dictionary, and write down the definitions for each.

THE ANCIENT AMERICAN WORLD

CRITICAL THINKING
CAUSE AND EFFECT

Read the chapter, and in your history journal create a cause and effect graphic organizer (see the T-chart on page 9 of this study guide). Below is a list of causes and effects from the chapter that relate to the Spanish conquest and destruction of the Inca Empire. Match the causes with their effects in the columns of your graphic organizer.

CAUSE	EFFECT
The Spaniards in Cajamarca could see light from thousands of Inca campfires on the hillsides,	SO Pizarro felt justified in slaughtering the unarmed Inca.
Spanish law required conquistadors to give native people a chance to accept Christianity before blood was shed,	SO Huayna Capac died of smallpox.
He had no immunity against disease brought by the Europeans,	SO his Inca warriors brought no weapons, and the armed Spaniards massacred 5,000 of them.
Atahualpa refused to accept Christianity,	SO they knew they were hugely outnumbered.
Atahualpa believed the Spaniards' claim that they came in peace,	SO a friar with a cross and prayer book met Atahualpa and his procession.

COMPREHENSION

Answer the following questions in your history journal using complete sentences:

1. What strategy for conquering native peoples had Francisco Pizarro learned from his cousin, Hernán Cortés?
2. Why did Atahualpa make the terrible mistake of believing Pizarro's claim that he and his soldiers had come in peace?
3. Why did Atahualpa agree, just before the Spaniards strangled him, to convert to Christianity?

ALL OVER THE MAP

On the map, write in the locations and geographical features listed below.

- Cuzco
- Andes Mountains
- Cajamarca
- Pacific Ocean
- Quito

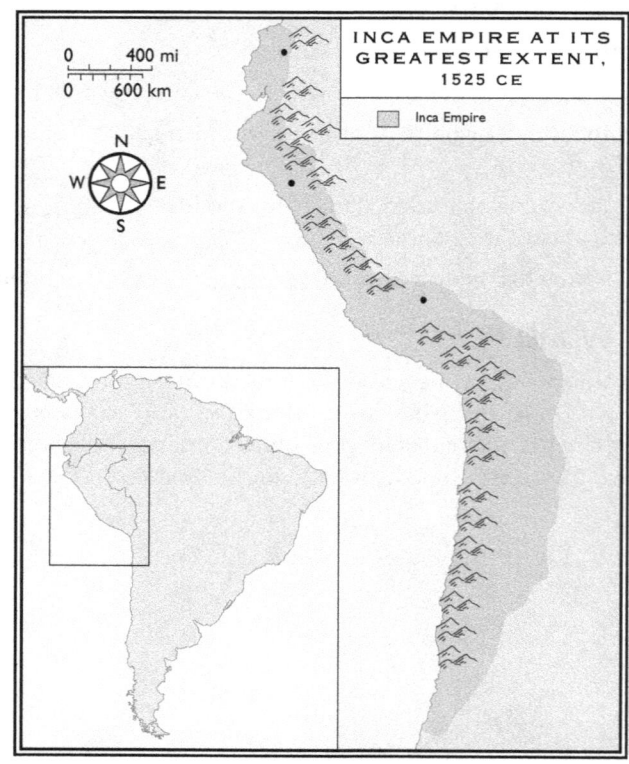

36   CHAPTER 13

CHAPTER 14: ROLLER-COASTER ROADS: UP AND DOWN THE ANDEAN WORLD

CHAPTER SUMMARY

Pedro de Cieza de León, a Spaniard, spent 16 years traveling in the Andes Mountains. He wrote a chronicle that described their geography and helped scholars understand the lives of ancient Andeans.

ACCESS

In his *Chronicle of Peru*, Pedro de Cieza de León tried to describe everything he could about the Andes Mountain region and the people living there. What different kinds of things did he see? As you read the chapter, create a list in your history journal of 10 different things he described in his book. Look for details about the people, their houses, their habits, the foods they ate, the land, the weather, and animals.

CAST OF CHARACTERS

Write three adjectives that describe Pedro de Cieza de León.

_____

WHAT HAPPENED WHEN?

In your history journal, copy the timeline graphic organizer on page 9 of this study guide. Then arrange the following dates from the chapter chronologically from top to bottom on the timeline, then briefly describe what happened during these approximate dates in the corresponding boxes.

January 9, 1534   March 1535   1541   1548   1549   1550

WORD BANK

condor   manioc   ingot

Fill in the blanks with the correct words from the Word Bank. One word is not used.

1. The Andean people harvested and ate _____, a root that grows in rain forests.

2. A _____ is an Andean vulture.

WORD PLAY

1. Look up in a dictionary the word you didn't use. Write a sentence using that word.

   _____

2. The word *chronicle* comes from the Greek word *chronos*, which means "time." In a dictionary, find three other words that begin with *chron* or *chrono*. Write the words and their definitions in your history journal, then write a sentence using each word.

THE ANCIENT AMERICAN WORLD

COMPREHENSION
SEQUENCE OF EVENTS

Read the story of how Pedro de Cieza de León came to South America, then use the sequence of events graphic organizer on page 9 of this study guide to organize the following events from the story in the correct order.

- Six years after Cieza de León landed in South America, he started writing his book about Peru.
- Cieza de León left Seville when he was 13 years old.
- Cieza de León watched with astonishment as Spanish soldiers unloaded silver and gold from a ship that had been to South America.
- Cieza de León wanted to see South America for himself.
- Cieza de León's parents arranged the trip to South America for him.

Answer the following questions in your history journal, using complete sentences:

1. What were the two goals of the captain and crew with whom Cieza de Léon traveled to South America?
2. Compared with other European chroniclers of the Spanish conquest, what was different about the way Cieza de Léon described the South American people and their customs?
3. What is distinctive about Lake Titicaca?

OUTLINE

How did the Andean family groups called *ayllus* learn to manage the land to their benefit? Use the outline graphic organizer on page 8 of this study guide to gain understanding of what they did to survive and thrive. Write the main idea of the outline at the top of the page, and then fill in several details from the chapter beneath each of the following topics:

Topic I: What *ayllus* were

Topic II: How *ayllus* survived on the Pacific coast and in coastal deserts

Topic III: How *ayllus* managed the land around Lake Titicaca

Topic IV: How *ayllus* benefited from the rain forest

Topic V: How *ayllus* stored and managed extra food

1. What animal did *ayllus* use to haul goods?_____
2. What do these animals do if they are loaded with more than about 100 pounds to carry?_____

ALL OVER THE MAP

On the map, write in the geographical features listed below.

- Pacific Ocean
- Lake Titicaca
- Andes Mountains
- Supe River
- Amazon River
- Moche River

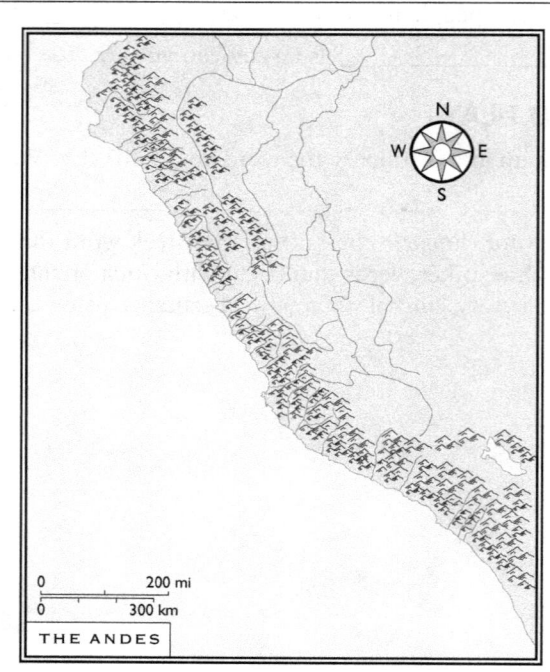

38 CHAPTER 14

CHAPTER 15
A TALE OF TWO CITIES: THE OLDEST TOWNS IN THE AMERICAS

CHAPTER SUMMARY
Archaeologists are excavating and studying the ancient settlements of Aspero and Caral, in Peru, to determine whether they were cities or ceremonial centers.

ACCESS
Aspero and Caral are ancient settlements with similarities and also some striking differences. Create a Venn diagram in your history journal with two circles, similar to the graphic organizer on page 9 of this study guide. In one circle write *Aspero*, and in the other write *Caral*. As you read the chapter, write the archaeological discoveries listed below in the appropriate circles. Any finds that the cities have in common should be written in the space where the circles overlap.

- Cottonseeds, cotton fibers, or cloth
- Bones and shells of seafood
- Traces of squash and beans
- Living quarters and household trash
- Irrigation canal
- Flat-topped mounds
- Corpses
- No evidence of planted crops
- Sunken plazas

CAST OF CHARACTERS
Briefly describe the significance of these characters:

Francisco Pizarro _____

Ruth Shady _____

WHAT HAPPENED WHEN?
Use the timeline on page 119 in the chapter to help you answer the following questions:
1. When did people begin building plazas? _____
2. When was the first high mound built in Aspero? _____
3. When did archaeologists partly excavate Aspero? _____

WORD BANK
sunken   ceremonial   colossal   corrosive

Complete the sentences below with the correct words from the Word Bank. One word is not used.
1. The _____ Andean mountains are huge and breathtaking.
2. The ruins at Caral are being destroyed by _____ rain, wind, and air pollution.
3. Many low-level, or _____, plazas were found in the ruins at Caral.

WORD PLAY
To create cloth, a weaver lays out *vertical* warp threads and then weaves *horizontal* weft threads over and under the warp threads. What are the meanings of *vertical* and *horizontal*? In your history journal, write the dictionary definition for each word. Then draw a vertical line and a horizontal line, and label each.

THE ANCIENT AMERICAN WORLD

COMPREHENSION

SEQUENCE OF EVENTS

Read the description on page 116 of how archaeologists believe Pirámide Mayor was constructed, then use the sequence of events graphic organizer on page 9 of this study guide to organize the following steps in the correct order:

- The builders eventually packed the inside walls with more than 7 million cubic feet of rock.
- They made small mesh bags from reeds and filled them with loose rubble.
- People cut rocks with stone tools.
- They plastered the walls and painted them red.
- They piled up rocks to make walls around the base of the pyramid.

MULTIPLE CHOICE

Answer the following questions:

1. What do archaeologists believe may have happened to the people whose corpses were found in one of the mounds?
    a. They died of disease.   b. They died accidentally.   c. They were sacrificed to the gods.

2. What are the oldest crafts in the Andean world?
    a. pottery making   b. spinning thread and weaving cloth   c. jewelry making

3. What particular kind of seafood did the people of Aspera eat a lot of?
    a. anchovies   b. shark   c. squid

4. How many people have to live in an ancient settlement for it to be called a city?
    a. 10,000   b. 60   c. 1,800

5. What kinds of evidence would tell archaeologists that Aspero and Carval were cities?
    a. maps   b. a large number of houses and many kinds of tools   c. written histories

6. Why don't archaeologists know for sure whether Aspero and Carval were cities?
    a. They didn't find human remains.   c. They didn't find housing.
    b. They haven't been able to fully excavate the huge sites.

7. Why is Ruth Shady concerned about the ruins in Caral?
    _____

8. What does she hope the discoveries in Caral will help the people of Peru remember?
    _____

ALL OVER THE MAP

On the map, write in the geographical features listed below.

- Pacific Ocean
- Supe River
- Caral
- Aspero
- Peru

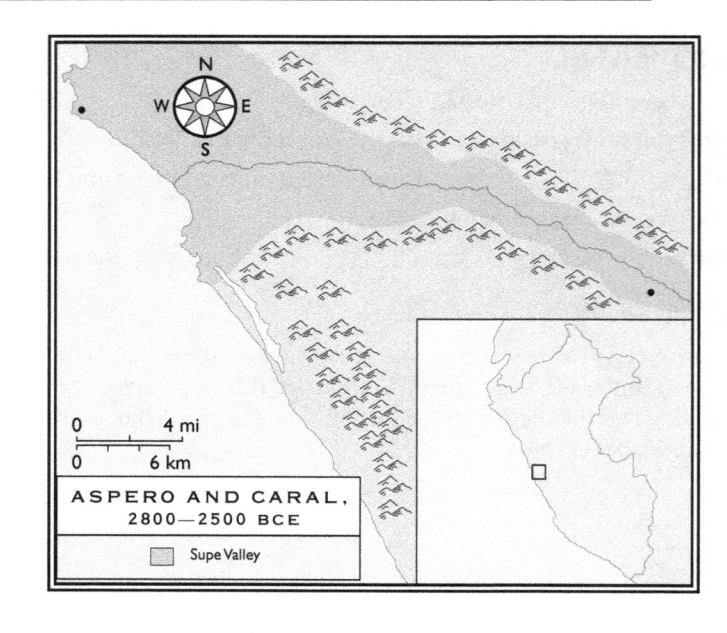

CHAPTER 15

CHAPTER 16

THE THUNDEROUS TEMPLE: ANDEAN PEOPLE CONNECT

CHAPTER SUMMARY

People came from many different Peruvian cultures to the temple in Chavín de Huántar to make offerings to their supreme god and to ask questions of the oracle. The sacred animal imagery of their ancient religion can be seen in the arts and crafts of the time.

ACCESS

How did ancient Andean pilgrims prepare themselves to visit a temple? What types of offerings did they make to their gods? What might their worship experiences have been like? Use the K-W-L graphic organizer on page 8 of this study guide to help you learn more. In the *What I Know* column, write what you already know about the religious practices of ancient Andeans. (If you don't know anything yet, that's okay.) Fill in the *What I Want to Know* column with your questions. As you read the chapter, write the answers to your questions and other interesting facts in the *What I Learned* column.

CAST OF CHARACTERS

What do archaeologists Luis Lubreras and Richard Burger suspect about the sewer system in the temple at Chavín?

_____

WHAT HAPPENED WHEN?

5000 BCE _____

2000 BCE _____

1900 BCE _____

400 BCE _____

1976 CE _____

WORD BANK

alloy   oracle   batik

Fill in the blanks with the correct words from the Word Bank. One word is not used.

1. An _____ is a mixture of metals.

2. To _____ fabric, weavers would coat areas of the fabric with a waterproof substance, then dye the fabric to create a design.

WORD PLAY

Look *batik* up in a dictionary and answer the following questions:

1. What language does *batik* come from? _____

2. How is *batik* pronounced? Write the phonetic spelling here and say the word aloud to a friend.
   _____

3. Look up the word not used in the Word Bank. Write a sentence using that word.
   _____

WORKING WITH PRIMARY SOURCES

The Lanzón sculpture, Chavín de Huántar, 400 BCE

What did the Lanzón sculpture look like? What were the sacred meanings of its imagery? Use the outline graphic organizer on page 8 of this study guide to understand what the sculpture may have meant to the Andean pilgrims. Write the main idea of the outline at the top of the page, and then fill in several details from the chapter beneath each of the following topics:

Topic I: The shape and dimensions of the Lanzón sculpture

Topic II: The designs carved on the sculpture

Topic III: How the sculpture may be a link to east and west, the heavens and the underworld

COMPREHENSION

Answer the following questions, using complete sentences:

1. How did the religion at Chavín serve as a connection between different Peruvian cultures?
   _____
   _____
   _____

2. What were the benefits of being a temple priest?
   _____
   _____
   _____

3. What kinds of animals did Peruvian craftspeople use in their designs?
   _____
   _____
   _____

GROUP TOGETHER

Wouldn't it be interesting to know what other students think about the ways the Andeans showed their devotion to the gods? Is their religion similar to any other religions, ancient or modern? Get a few friends together and ask your teacher to help you organize a discussion group at school. Have one person take notes and another person present the group's ideas to the class.

CHAPTER 17
ON TOP OF THE WORLD: HIGHLAND EMPIRES IN THE ANDES

CHAPTER SUMMARY

With a population of as many as 34,000, Tiwanaku, on Lake Titicaca, was the largest city in the ancient Andean world. Four hundred miles to the northeast, farmers in the city of Wari built innovative stone irrigation canals on steep mountain slopes. The ruins of both cities reveal the religious and architectural influence of Chavín.

ACCESS

Read the description of the Bearded Statue on pages 128–129 in the chapter, then answer the following questions in your history journal, using complete sentences:

1. Where in the plaza at Tiwanaku did the Bearded Statue originally stand?
2. What does the Bearded Statue hold in its hands?
3. How is the Bearded Statue similar to the Staff God of Chavín?
4. In modern Quechua-speaking communities, what does a staff represent?

CAST OF CHARACTERS

When was Pedro de Cieza de León's journal published? _____

WHAT HAPPENED WHEN?

Use the timeline on page 132 in the chapter to help you answer the following questions:

1. When was Tiwanaku established on Lake Titicaca? _____
2. When did people invent raised fields around Lake Titicaca? _____
3. When did drought destroy Tiwanaku? _____

GO FIGURE

How many years passed between the invention of raised fields around Lake Titicaca and the destruction of Tiwanaku by drought? _____

WORD BANK

wither   grimacing   metropolis   preside

Complete the sentences below with the correct words from the Word Bank. One word is not used.

1. The _____ of Tiwanaku was the largest city in the ancient Andean world.
2. Crops _____ when they don't get enough water.
3. The sunken square plaza at Tiwanaku was surrounded by statues of _____ stone heads.

THE ANCIENT AMERICAN WORLD

WORD PLAY

According to the chapter, what are two other ways that *Tiwanaku* can be spelled?

_____

CRITICAL THINKING

COMPARE AND CONTRAST

The ancient cities of Tiwanaku and Wari have some similarities and their own unique characteristics, too. Create a Venn diagram with two circles in your history journal, similar to the graphic organizer on page 9 of this study guide. In one circle write *Tiwanaku*, and in the other write *Wari*. As you read the chapter, write the descriptions listed below in the appropriate circles. Any features the cities share should be written in the space where the circles overlap.

- Multistory apartment buildings
- Sunken square plaza
- Terraced mountainside fields for crops
- New walls built with ancient stones
- The Bearded Statue
- Evidence of feasts and parties
- Raised fields for crops
- Mountainside irrigation canals
- Pottery with images of the Staff God
- Underground drains and channels

COMPREHENSION

SEQUENCE OF EVENTS

The sidebar on page 131 tells the Inca story of the creation of the world. Read the story, then copy the sequence of events graphic organizer on page 9 of this study guide in your history journal. Organize these events in the correct order:

- The creator went to Tiwanaku and modeled animals and people out of clay.
- The creator ordered the tribes of people to go into caves, lakes, and hills.
- The creator made the world but left it in darkness.
- The creator told the tribes to emerge and settle in their assigned places.
- The jealous sun threw ashes in the moon's brighter face and dimmed her light.
- The creator painted clothes on the tribes of people and gave them food, language and songs.
- The creator caused the sun and moon to emerge from an island in Lake Titicaca.

READ MORE

To read more about the Inca world, see the Further Reading suggestions at the end of *The Ancient American World*.

CHAPTER 18
THE MAN WITH THE GOLD EARRINGS: MOCHE ARTISTS IN COASTAL PERU

CHAPTER SUMMARY
Meticulously detailed gold jewelry and sculpted pottery found in pyramids in Sipán, Peru, show that the artists of the Moche kingdom were the finest craftsmen in the ancient Andean world.

ACCESS
As you read the chapter, answer the following questions in your history journal, using complete sentences:

1. Why didn't archaeologists think that the pyramids at Sipán were worth their time?
2. What made archaeologists decide to go ahead and excavate the small pyramid?
3. What did the makers' marks on the Moche pyramid bricks probably mean?

CAST OF CHARACTERS
Describe the significance of the following characters:

Walter Alva _____

Christopher Donnan _____

WHAT HAPPENED WHEN?
100 CE _____

16th century CE _____

1986 CE _____

WORD BANK
confetti   honeycomb   runt   goldsmith

Complete the sentences below with the correct words from the Word Bank. One word is not used.

1. The 40-foot-high pyramid at Sipán was a _____ compared to the gigantic ones located at Cerro Blanco.
2. A _____ creates art with precious metals.
3. The tiny warrior statues found at Sipán had assistants carved from chips of turquoise the size of _____.

THE ANCIENT AMERICAN WORLD

CRITICAL THINKING

OUTLINE

What did archaeologists find in the small pyramid at Sipán? Read the story of the excavation on pages 135–137 in the chapter, then create an outline graphic organizer in your history journal similar to the one on page 8 of this study guide. Write the main idea of the outline at the top of the page, and then fill in several details from the chapter beneath each of the following topics:

Topic I: The discoveries of the first chamber

Topic II: What was in the eight-foot-by-ten-foot room

Topic III: The warrior earrings

Topic IV: The other human and animal remains

CAUSE AND EFFECT

In your history journal create a cause and effect graphic organizer (see the T-chart on page 9 of this study guide). Listed below are causes and effects from the chapter that relate to the Moche people and the archaeological discoveries at Sipán. Match the causes with their effects in the columns of your graphic organizer.

CAUSE	EFFECT
Walter Alva had seen many owl-headed priests on Moche pottery,	SO they knew that the crumpled skeleton with bent knees and arms had probably been sacrificed.
They thought the warrior-priest must have been an important person,	SO we know that he probably died a natural death.
The warrior-priest's bones weren't fractured,	SO they hacked many holes in the small pyramid.
Looters were looking for gold to steal,	SO the archaeologists named him the "Lord of Sipán."
The excavators knew that the Moche usually lay their dead on their backs when they buried them,	SO he knew that the Moche admired desert owls.

WITH A PARENT OR PARTNER

How have other cultures around the world explained the mystery of creation? With a parent or older family member, do an Internet search using the phrase "creation myths." Find an interesting myth from another culture and read it with your parent or family member. Then write out the myth in your own words on a page in your history journal.

HISTORY JOURNAL

Don't forget to share your history journal with your classmates, and ask if you can see what their journals look like. You might be surprised—and get some new ideas.

CHAPTER 19
CHAN CHAN: CAPITAL CITY OF THE ANDEAN KINGDOM OF CHIMOR

CHAPTER SUMMARY

The pre-Inca Chimú people built the city of Chan Chan and controlled over 600 miles of coastal Peru until they were conquered and absorbed by the Inca.

ACCESS

What special kinds of tasks did Chimú nobles perform for their kings? To explore the subject, create a main idea map graphic organizer in your history journal similar to the one on page 8 of this study guide. In the large central circle, write *The King*. Read the sidebar on page 142, *The Care and Feeding of a King*, and then in seven smaller connecting circles write the descriptive titles of the nobles who served the Chimú kings.

CAST OF CHARACTERS

In your history journal write a descriptive sentence about each of the following characters from the chapter:

Taycanamu (tay-cah-NAH-mu)   Allan Kolata

Geoffrey Conrad   Miguel Cabello

WHAT HAPPENED WHEN?

635 CE _____
900 CE _____
1465 CE _____
1470 CE _____
1604 CE _____

WORD BANK

labyrinth   famine   anonymous   handiwork

Complete the sentences below with the correct words from the Word Bank. One word is not used.

1. If someone is _____, that person's name is unknown.

2. The courtyards in the Chan Chan compounds were connected by a _____, or maze, of passages.

3. According to legend, the early Chimú people were cursed by floods and a year of food shortages, or _____,.

WORD PLAY

What is a *labyrinth*? Look the word up in a dictionary and write the definition in your history journal. Then use the word in a complete sentence.

CRITICAL THINKING
FACT OR OPINION?

A fact is a statement that can be proved. An opinion is a statement that can neither be proved nor disproved. Read the chapter, and for each statement below about the Chimú and the excavation of their palaces, write "F" or "O" to indicate whether it is a fact or an opinion.

_____ There may have been 10 kings of Chimor.

_____ The Chimú built Chan Chan in 900 CE.

_____ The Chimú probably started the custom of "split inheritance" used by the Inca.

_____ The fortresslike construction of the palace compounds would have made ancient visitors feel unsettled.

_____ Every compound had large, aboveground wells.

_____ U-shaped adobe storerooms were probably used to store goods paid to Chan Chan as tribute.

_____ By 1450, Chan Chan was the second-largest city in the Andean world.

_____ When a ruler of Chimor died, his body was mummified and buried.

Briefly explain in your history journal the Chimú and Inca custom of "split inheritance."

COMPREHENSION

Answer the following questions in your history journal, using complete sentences:

1. Do historians know how many kings ruled Chimor?
2. What was the advantage of having only one door leading into a palace compound?
3. How do archaeologists know that animals lived in the kitchens of the Chimú craftspeople?
4. What objects have excavators found buried with rulers of Chimor?
5. Why did ancient Andeans bury items like clothes and jewelry with people who died?

ALL OVER THE MAP

On the map on page, write in the geographical features listed below.

- Pacific Ocean
- Tiwanaku
- Sipán
- Wari
- Andes
- Lake Titicaca
- Chavín
- Moche
- Cerro Blanco
- Moche River
- Chan Chan

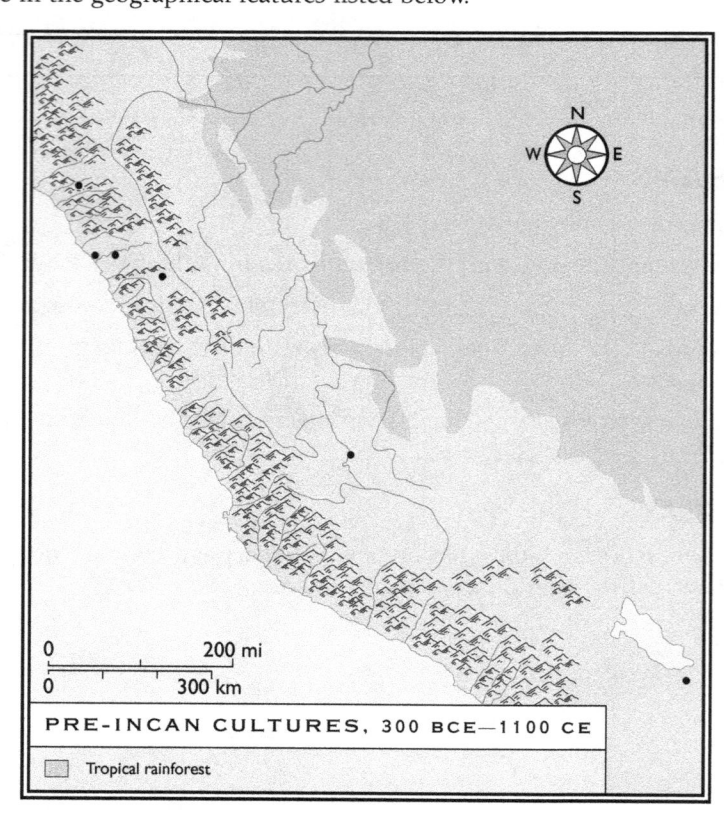

PRE-INCAN CULTURES, 300 BCE—1100 CE

Tropical rainforest

CHAPTER 20
CUZCO RULES: THE INCA IN THE LAND OF THE FOUR QUARTERS

CHAPTER SUMMARY

Like Aztec ruler Itzcoatl, Inca emperor Pachacuti rewrote history and proclaimed himself to be a descendant of the gods. The Inca Empire borrowed many of its traditions from previous cultures.

ACCESS

How did Pachacuti become emperor, and what sort of ruler was he? In your history joural, copy the K-W-L graphic organizer on page 8 of this study guide to help you learn more. In the *What I Know* column, write what you already know about the Inca Empire under Pachacuti. (If you don't know anything yet, that's okay.) Fill in the *What I Want to Know* column with your questions. As you read the chapter, write the answers to your questions and other interesting facts in the *What I Learned* column.

CAST OF CHARACTERS

In your history journal, write a descriptive sentence about each of the following characters from the chapter:

Pachacuti (pah-chah-KOO-tee)

Topa Inca

Huayna Capac (WHY-nah KAH-pahk)

Bernabé Cobo

WHAT HAPPENED WHEN?

Using the timeline graphic organizer on page 9, arrange the following dates from the chapter chronologically from top to bottom on the timeline, then briefly describe what happened during these approximate dates in the corresponding boxes.

1438 CE   1569 CE   1460–1470 CE   1653 CE

750 CE   1471 CE   1926 CE

WORD BANK

insignificant   addictive   divine   slingshot

Complete the sentences below with the correct words from the Word Bank. One word is not used.

1. When Pachacuti claimed he was descended from the Sun God Inti, he made himself part of a _____ family.

2. A weapon used for hurling rocks is a _____.

3. Cuzco was an unimportant, _____ place in the Andean world.

WORD PLAY

What is the English translation of the Quechua word *Tawantinsuyu*?

_____

THE ANCIENT AMERICAN WORLD

CRITICAL THINKING
SUMMARIZING

The Inca borrowed traditions and ways of doing things from other cultures. Read the chapter and explain in your history journal using complete sentences how the Inca borrowed or improved on the practices or inventions of these cultures:

> Wari
>
> Chavín and Tiwanahu
>
> *ayllus*
>
> Chimú

OUTLINE

What was a *khipu*, and how did it help the emperor keep track of the produce and trade goods in his empire? Read the description of *khipus* on page 151, then create an outline graphic organizer in your history journal similar to the one on page 8 of this study guide. Write the main idea of the outline at the top of the page, and then fill in several details from the chapter beneath each of the following topics:

Topic I: Where and when *khipus* were discovered, and what they looked like

Topic II: The meanings of the knots

Topic III: The emperor and the *Khiupukamayoq*

COMPREHENSION

Answer the following questions, using complete sentences:

1. How did Pachacuti use the sons of local rulers to ensure that he wasn't cheated out of his taxes?
   _____
   _____
   _____

2. Why couldn't the ancient Peruvians pay their taxes with money?
   _____
   _____
   _____

3. How were goods moved quickly across the Inca Empire?
   _____
   _____
   _____

READ MORE

To read more about the Inca, see the Further Reading suggestions at the end of *The Ancient American World*.

> **HISTORY JOURNAL**
>
> *Don't forget to share your history journal with your classmates, and ask if you can see what their journals look like. You might be surprised—and get some new ideas.*

CHAPTER 21
CHOSEN GIRLS AND BREECHCLOTH BOYS: LIFE IN THE INCA EMPIRE

CHAPTER SUMMARY
Young Inca children helped their parents with household chores and work in the fields and played games. At age 10 some girls were selected for sacrifice, others to train for specific societal duties. Other girls were expected to marry. Boys celebrated maturity at age 14.

ACCESS
What was life like for Inca children? To answer this question, create a main idea map graphic organizer in your history journal similar to the one on page 8 of this study guide. In the large central circle, write *Inca Children at Work and Play*. Read the first two pages of the chapter, and fill at least 10 smaller connecting circles with brief descriptions of the kinds of chores Inca children were expected to help with and the games they played.

CAST OF CHARACTERS
Although Bernabé Cobo was Spanish and Guamán Poma was Inca, what did they have in common? _____
(Hint: The answer is in the descriptive words about each man on page 154.)

WHAT HAPPENED WHEN?
Briefly describe what happened on the following dates:
1493 _____
1527 _____

WORD BANK
mutiny   pestilence   sibling   famished

Complete the sentences below with the correct words from the Word Bank. One word is not used.

1. A _____ is a brother or sister.
2. At puberty, Inca girls who were not Chosen Women were _____ after fasting from food for two days.
3. Emperor Huayna Capac died of the _____ that was the smallpox virus.

CRITICAL THINKING
COMPARE AND CONTRAST
At age 10, Inca girls were assigned specific roles and duties in society. Listed below are the duties and expectations they faced, depending on whether they were a Chosen Woman, a Mama Kona, or a "left-out." Create a Venn diagram in your history journal with three circles, similar to the graphic organizer on page 9 of this study guide. In one circle write *Chosen Woman*, in another write *Mama Kona*, and in the third write *Left-Out*. As you read pages 154–156, write the descriptions listed below in the appropriate circles. Any features shared by the different roles should be written in the spaces where the circles overlap.

THE ANCIENT AMERICAN WORLD   **51**

- lived in a compound with other girls and women
- learned cooking, brewing *chicha*, spinning, weaving, and sewing
- spent four years away from their families
- after puberty, could be reclassified for sacrifice
- became a Mama Kona after puberty
- remained in the compound to teach young girls
- cared for shrines
- prepared festival foods
- could never marry
- could never speak to a man again
- was expected to marry
- at puberty, underwent a two-day fasting ritual followed by a feast
- was given a grown-up name

If a Mama Kona was caught talking to a man, how was she punished?

___

COMPREHENSION

SEQUENCE OF EVENTS

Inca men and women were expected to marry but had to have the approval of the commander of their district. Read the descriptions of engagement and marriage on pages 156–157 in the chapter, then use the sequence of events graphic organizer on page 9 of this study guide to organize the following events in the correct order:

- The groom and his family visited the bride's home, where he placed a sandal on her foot.
- The wedding ended with a feast.
- The district commander placed the young men in a line facing the young women.
- The bride gave the groom clothes and a gold or silver ornament.
- A man pointed to his future bride, and she stood behind him.
- The bride's and groom's parents gave them gifts and advice.
- If two men wanted the same woman, the commander made the decision in the name of the emperor.

GROUP TOGETHER

Wouldn't it be interesting to talk with other students about what life was like as a child in ancient Peru? In particular, think about these questions.

1. How do you think the parents of a child chosen by Inca officials for sacrifice might have understood and lived with their loss?

2. If you were an Inca girl, which would you rather be, a Mama Kona or a "left-out"? Why?

Get a few friends together and ask your teacher to help you organize a discussion group at school. Have one person take notes and another person present the group's ideas to the class.

REPORTS AND SPECIAL PROJECTS

There's always more to find out about ancient America. Take a look at the Further Reading section at the end of the book (pages 163–165). Here you will find a number of books on different topics relating to ancient American history and culture. Many of them will be available in your school or local public library.

GETTING STARTED

Explore the Further Reading section for any of these reasons.

— You're curious and want to learn more about a particular topic.

— You want to do a research report on ancient America.

— You still have questions about something covered in the book.

— You need more information for a special classroom project.

What's the best way to find the books that will help you the most?

LOOK AT THE SUBHEADS

The books are organized by topic. The subhead Religion tells you where to find books on ancient American gods, for example. Go to Art to learn more about Aztec and Maya art. Let the subheads give you ideas for reports and special projects.

LOOK AT THE BOOK TITLES

The titles of the books can tell you a lot about what is inside. The books listed under Native Chronicles offer modern translations of ancient American poetry and legends.

LOOK FOR GENERAL REFERENCES

This section also lists general books, which are useful starting points for further research. General Works will list titles that provide a broad overview of ancient American history. Judge by the titles which books will be the most useful to you. Other references include:

— Dictionaries

— Encyclopedias

— Atlases

OTHER RESOURCES

Information comes in all kinds of formats. Use the book to learn about primary sources. Go to the library for videos, DVDs, and audio materials. And don't forget about the Internet!

AUDIO-VISUAL MATERIALS

Your school or local library can offer documentary videos and DVDs on ancient America, as well as audio materials. If you have access to a computer, explore the sites listed in the section titled Websites (page 166) for some good jumping-off points. These are organized by topic, with brief descriptions of what you will find on the site. Many websites list additional reading, as well as other Internet links you can visit.

What you have learned about the ancient American world so far is just a beginning. Learning more is an ongoing adventure!

LIBRARY / MEDIA CENTER RESEARCH LOG

NAME _____

DUE DATE _____

What I Need to **Find**

Brainstorm: Other Sources and Places to Look

Places I **Know** to Look

I need to use:
- ☐ primary sources.
- ☐ secondary

WHAT I FOUND

Title/Author/Location (call # or URL)

How I Found it
- Suggestion
- Library Catalog
- Browsing
- Internet Search
- Web link

- Primary Source
- Secondary Source

- Book/Periodical
- Website
- Other

Rate each source from 1 (low) to 4 (high) in the categories below
- helpful
- relevant

Mini Classics

Log Cabins

Contents

Log Cabin Star	2
Basket of Flowers	4
Pineapple Delight	5
Star in the Cabin	8
Cabin Glow	11
Corner Lot	12
Log Cabin Barn Raising	14
Half Log Cabin	15
Field and Furrows	16
Mini Stitching Tips	17

CHITRA PUBLICATIONS

Challenging

Shown on page 10

Designed by Ruth Nies Gordy

Log Cabin Star

Unique block placement will make your star shine!

QUILT SIZE 36" square
BLOCK SIZE 3 1/2" square

MATERIALS
Yardage is estimated for 44" fabric.
- 3/4 yard navy print for center star, border and binding
- 1/2 yard medium blue print
- 1/2 yard pink print
- 1 3/8 yards beige print
- 38" square backing fabric
- 38" square batting

CUTTING
Dimensions include 1/4" seam allowance.
- Cut 9: 1" x 44" strips, navy, for the star
- Cut 2: 2 1/2" x 32 1/2" strips, navy, for the outer border
- Cut 2: 2 1/2" x 36 1/2" strips, navy, for the outer border
- Cut 4: 1 3/4" x 44" strip, navy, for the binding
- Cut 15: 1" x 44" strips, medium blue
- Cut 15: 1" x 44" strips, pink
- Cut 38: 1" x 44" strips, beige
- Cut 2: 2 1/2" x 28 1/2" strips, beige, for the inner border
- Cut 2: 2 1/2" x 32 1/2" strips, beige, for the inner border

DIRECTIONS
- Log Cabin blocks are colored diagonally with one light side and one dark side. Sometimes each "log" is a different fabric, so a number of different darks are on one side and several different lights are on the other side. In this case, the blocks consist of only two fabrics; all the dark rows are the same print and all the light rows are the same print. Overall quilt designs are achieved by rotating the blocks and playing with the arrangement of lights and darks.

- To strip piece the beige/navy block, lay a 1" x 44" beige strip at right angles to a 1" x 44" navy strip right sides together. Stitch the strips together, as shown. Trim the excess fabric from each side, using the raw edges as a guide.

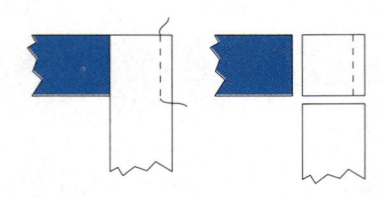

- Finger press the seam toward the navy fabric. Place the squares on the sewing machine, right side up, navy portion at top. Lay the 1" navy strip on top, right sides together and stitch to the end of the beige fabric. Trim away the excess fabric and finger press toward the navy.

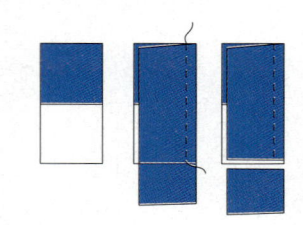

- Turn the block counter-clockwise on the sewing machine. Now the navy is across the top and the navy/beige is at the bottom.

- Lay the beige strip on top and stitch it to the end of the unit. Trim the excess fabric and finger press the seams outward.

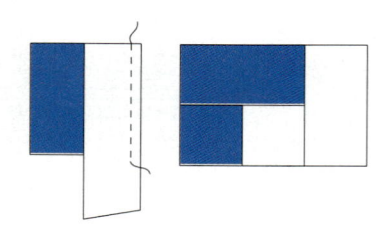

- Turn the block counter-clockwise.

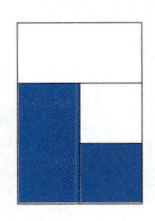

- Stitch a beige strip to the unit. Trim the excess fabric and finger press seams outward.

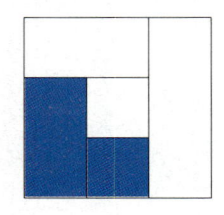

- Continue turning counter-clockwise, sewing 2 adjacent navy strips, then 2 adjacent beige strips, until the block is finished. Press all seams outward. Make 8.

**Block 1 • Make 8
Beige/Navy**

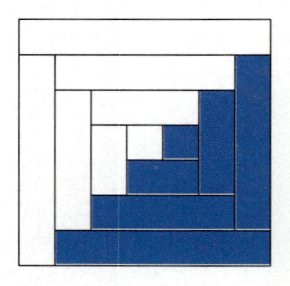

- This quilt consists of 64 blocks in 6 different fabric combinations. Complete all the blocks using the same method. See page 3 for additional block configurations.

- Lay out the blocks as shown in the Assembly Diagram. Pay close attention to the orientation of the light/dark sides of the blocks and their placement in the

Mini Classics: Log Cabins

overall pattern. Stitch the blocks into rows. Join the rows.
- Press seam allowances so the rows alternate. Stitch the rows together.
- Stitch the 2 1/2" x 28 1/2" beige strips to opposite sides of the quilt. Stitch the 2 1/2" x 32 1/2" beige strips to the remaining sides of the quilt.
- Stitch the 2 1/2" x 32 1/2" navy strips to opposite sides of the quilt. Stitch the 2 1/2" x 36 1/2" navy strips to the remaining sides of the quilt.
- Finish as described in *Mini Stitching Tips* using the 1 3/4" navy strips for the binding.

Quilting Design for Log Cabin Star

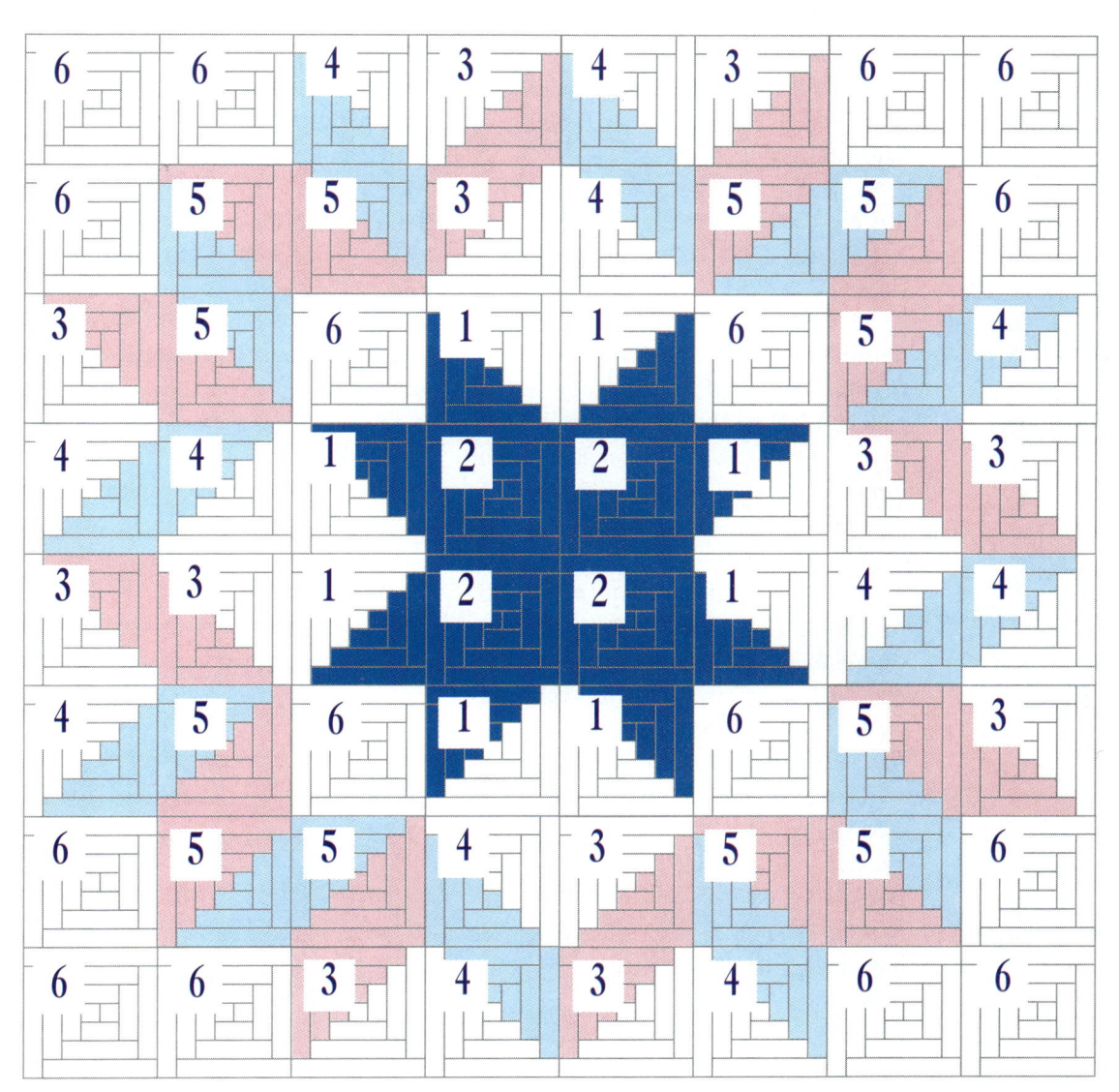

Block 2 • Make 4
Navy/Navy

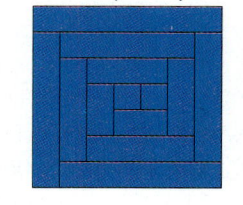

Block 3 • Make 12
Beige/Red

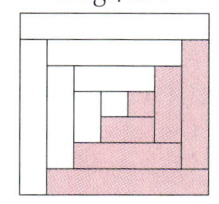

Block 4 • Make 12
Beige/Med. Blue

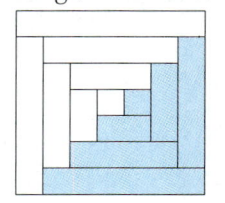

Block 5 • Make 12
Red/Med. Blue

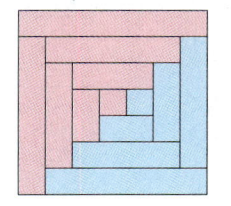

Block 6 • Make 16
Beige/Beige

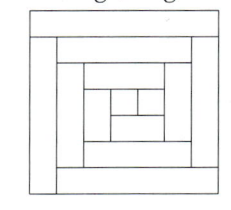

Assembly Diagram

Mini Classics: Log Cabins

Challenging

Shown on page 6

Basket of Flowers

A distinctive Log Cabin design!

QUILT SIZE 12 3/4" square
BLOCK SIZE 1 3/8" square

MATERIALS
Yardage is estimated for 44" fabric.
- 1/8 yard pink print
- 1/8 yard brown print
- 1/4 yard printed muslin
- 1/6 yard green
- 9" x 13" strip of floral print
- 14 3/4" square of backing fabric
- 14 3/4" square of thin batting
- 16" square of tracing paper or tear away interfacing

PREPARATION
- Cut 16: 4" squares of tracing paper
- Center each 4" square of tracing paper over the full-size Block Diagram. Trace all the lines and numbers on the squares.

Full-Size Block Diagram

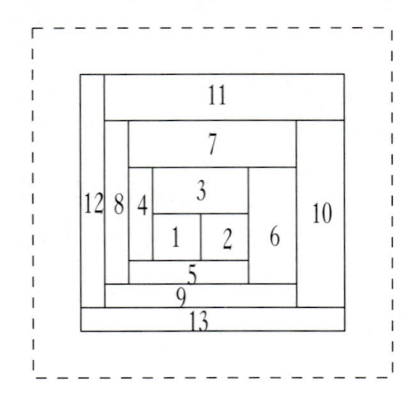

CUTTING
There are 4 blocks with different color combinations in this quilt. Cutting directions are given separately for each. Construction of each block is identical. Follow the sewing directions in Mini Stitching Tips. Fabric placement numbers are given with the cutting directions, noted on the tracing paper foundation and in the sewing directions. All dimensions include a 1/4" seam allowance.

Pink/Muslin (Make 6):
- Cut 18: 1" squares, muslin (logs 1, 4 & 5)
- Cut 12: 1" x 1 1/2" rectangles, muslin (logs 8 & 9)
- Cut 12: 1 1/2" x 2 1/2" rectangles, muslin (logs 12 & 13)
- Cut 12: 1" squares, pink (logs 2 & 3)
- Cut 12: 1" x 1 1/2" rectangles, pink (logs 6 & 7)
- Cut 12: 1 1/2" x 2 1/2" rectangles, pink (logs 10 & 11)

Muslin/Muslin (Make 5):
- Cut 25: 1" squares, muslin (logs 1, 2, 3, 4 & 5)
- Cut 20: 1" x 1 1/2" rectangles, muslin (logs 6, 7, 8 & 9)
- Cut 20: 1 1/2" x 2 1/2" rectangles, muslin (logs 10, 11, 12 & 13)

Brown/Muslin (Make 4):
- Cut 12: 1" squares, muslin (logs 1, 4 & 5)
- Cut 8: 1" x 1 1/2" rectangles, muslin (logs 8 & 9)
- Cut 8: 1 1/2" x 2 1/2" rectangles, muslin (logs 12 & 13)
- Cut 8: 1" squares, brown (logs 2 & 3)
- Cut 8: 1" x 1 1/2" rectangles, brown (logs 6 & 7)
- Cut 8: 1 1/2" x 2 1/2" rectangles, brown (logs 10 & 11)

Brown/Brown (Make 1):
- Cut 5: 1" squares, brown (logs 1, 2, 3, 4 & 5)
- Cut 4: 1" x 1 1/2" rectangles, brown (logs 6, 7, 8 & 9)
- Cut 4: 1 1/2" x 2 1/2" rectangles, brown (logs 10, 11, 12 & 13)

Also:
- Cut 2: 4 3/4" squares, muslin, then cut them each in half diagonally
- Cut 2: 1 1/8" x 8 1/4" strips, green
- Cut 2: 1 1/8" x 9 1/2" strips, green
- Cut 2: 1 3/4" x 44" strips, green, for binding
- Cut 2: 2" x 9 1/2" strips, floral print
- Cut 2: 2" x 12 1/2" strips, floral print

DIRECTIONS
- Refer to *Mini Stitching Tips* and follow directions for construction of each block using the 16 tracing paper foundations. Sewing directions refer to the fabric (log) placement by number. Cross reference the cutting and sewing directions with the log numbers.
- Complete 16 blocks.

FINISHING
- Lay out the blocks in 4 rows of 4 referring to the photo to create the flower basket. Stitch the blocks into rows along the last seamline on the foundation. Join the rows in the same manner.
- Remove the paper foundations carefully.
- Press lightly on the back.
- Stitch a muslin triangle to opposite sides of the center basket.
- Stitch a muslin triangle to the remaining sides of the center basket.
- Press and square to 8 1/4", if necessary.

Continued on page 5

Assembly Diagram

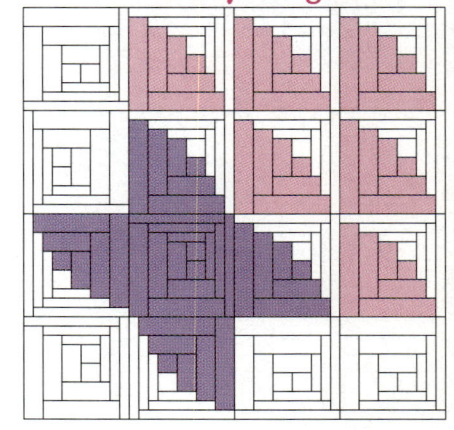

Intermediate

Shown on page 7

Pineapple Delight

A fabric confection! Perfect blocks are easy when you sew on foundation squares.

QUILT SIZE 15" square
BLOCK SIZE 3" square

MATERIALS
Yardage is estimated for 44" fabric.
• Scraps of aqua, purple and light prints for blocks
• 5" x 12" piece of pink for the inner border and block center
• 5" x 12" piece of light print for the middle border
• 1/4 yard aqua for the outer border
• 17" square of backing fabric
• 17" square of batting (optional)
• 15" square of tearaway interfacing

CUTTING
All dimensions include 1/4" seam allowance.
• Cut 9: 5" squares, tearaway interfacing
• Cut 9: 1" squares, pink, for position 1, the center
• Cut 2: 7/8" x 9 1/2" strips, pink, for the inner border
• Cut 2: 7/8" x 10 1/4" strips, pink, for the inner border
• Cut 2: 7/8" x 10 1/4" strips, light print, for the middle border
• Cut 2: 7/8" x 11" strips, light print, for the middle border
• Cut 2: 2 1/2" x 11" strips, aqua, for the outer border
• Cut 2: 2 1/2" x 15" strips, aqua, for the outer border
• Cut 2: 1 3/4" x 44" strips, aqua, for the binding

DIRECTIONS
• Center a 5" square of tearaway interfacing on the block diagram. Trace the block on the square using a permanent marker or pencil. Repeat for each of the 9 squares. Trace all lines and numbers. Follow the directions in *Mini Stitching Tips* for sewing on foundations.
• Attach strips in numerical order beginning with the 1" pink squares for the center. Use light print for positions 2, 5, 8, 11, and 14. Use aqua print for positions 3, 6, 9, 12, 15 and 17. Use purple print for positions 4, 7, 10, 13, 16 and 18.
• Press the completed blocks. Square each block to 3 1/2".
• Lay out the 9 blocks in 3 rows of 3, referring to the photo for placement. Stitch the blocks into rows then join the rows to complete the top.
• Remove the tearaway interfacing starting in the center. This step is optional but if you do, be very careful not to rip the fabric or pull the stitching.
• Stitch the 7/8" x 9 1/2" pink strips to opposite sides of the quilt top.
• Stitch the 7/8" x 10 1/4" pink strips to the remaining sides of the quilt.
• Stitch the 7/8" x 10 1/4" light print strips to opposite sides of the quilt. Stitch the 7/8" x 11" muslin strips to the remaining sides of the quilt top.
• Join the last border in a similar manner, first stitching the 2 1/2" x 11" aqua strips to the opposite sides and then the 2 1/2" x 15" aqua strips to the remaining sides of the quilt top.
• Batting is optional. Because of all the seams and the foundation square you may want to eliminate the batting.
• Finish as described in *Mini Stitching Tips*, using the 1 3/4" aqua strips for binding.

Full-Size Block for Pineapple Delight

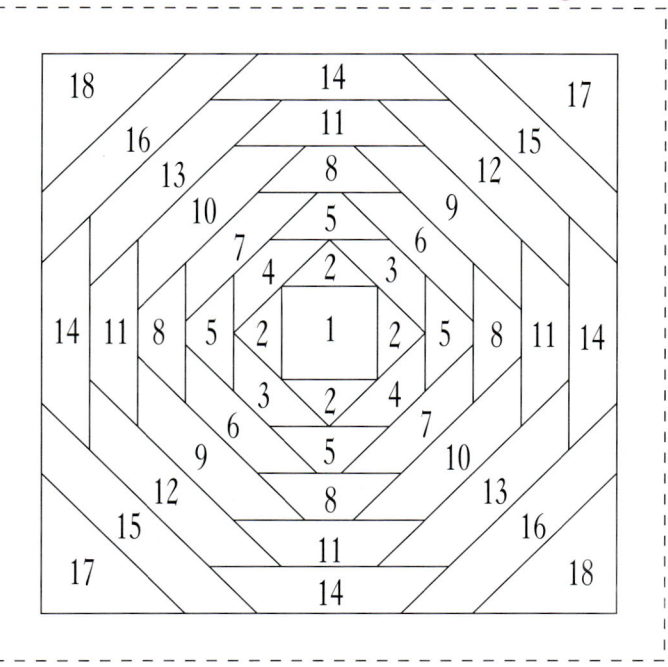

Basket of Flowers

• Stitch the 1 1/8" x 8 1/4" green strips to opposite sides of the quilt.
• Stitch the 1 1/8" x 9 1/2" green strips to the remaining sides of the quilt.

• Stitch the 2" x 9 1/2" floral print strips to opposite sides of the quilt.
• Stitch the 2" x 12 1/2" floral print strips to the remaining sides of the quilt.

• Finish as described in *Mini Stitching Tips*, using the 1 3/4" green strips for binding.

*Create a dramatic miniature Log Cabin by using contrasting fabrics. The large scale floral print gives motion when used in 1/4" strips. This hand pieced **"Field and Furrows"** quilt (8 1/2" x 10 1/2") by Joanne Nolt of Windham, Pennsylvania, became her "take along" piece for the winter. Pattern on page 16.*

*This Log Cabin miniature, **"Basket of Flowers"** (12 3/4" square) by Bonnie Jean Rosenbaum of Albuquerque, New Mexico, uses an off-center Log Cabin pattern with varying strip widths to create the curved effect. Pattern on page 4.*

Mini Classics: Log Cabins

Jacquelyn Conaway of Lafayette, Indiana, originally made **"Corner Lot"** (16 1/2" square) to put in her motor home. However, after piecing this little beauty, she found she wanted to enjoy it more than just on weekend camping trips. It is now hanging in her bedroom where she can view it daily! Pattern on page 12.

Shirley Conlon of San Diego, California, stitched her tiny **"Log Cabin Barn Raising"** (7" x 9 1/2") on foundations. These minuscule blocks are only 1 1/4" square! Shirley is a dollhouse enthusiast and makes quilts as well as cross-stitch and needlepoint items in miniature. Pattern on page 14.

Sheila Ekenstedt's **"Pineapple Delight"** (15" square) won third prize for "Other Techniques" in our 1992 Miniatures from the Heart Contest. To achieve perfect blocks, Sheila stitched them on a tear-away foundation. You can try the technique with our pattern on page 5.

Challenging

Shown on page 10

Star in the Cabin

Combine machine and hand piecing for this dramatic mini!

QUILT SIZE 18" x 21 1/4"
LOG CABIN BLOCK SIZE
1 3/4" square
STAR BLOCK SIZE 7 1/4" square

MATERIALS
Yardage is estimated for 44" fabric.
- 1/4 yard blue
- 1/8 yard ecru
- 3/4 yard beige print
- 1/2 yard tan print
- 1/4 yard medium brown
- 1/2 yard dark brown

CUTTING
Pattern pieces are full size and include 1/4" seam allowance, as do all dimensions given. The Log Cabin block was designed to be hand pieced using pattern pieces A through G in the color and placement indicated in the cutting directions that follow. If you would like to piece the block over a foundation, lay the full-size block face down on a light table and trace this reverse image on your foundation. Add 1/4" around the outside of the block. Make 56. Trace 12 half blocks in the same manner. Refer to Mini Stitching Tips *for detailed instructions on foundation piecing. Refer to the cutting directions for color placement.*

For each of 56 Log Cabin blocks:
- Cut 1: A, blue, for the center
- Cut 1: A, beige, position 1
- Cut 1: B, beige, position 2
- Cut 1: C, beige, position 5
- Cut 1: D, beige, position 6
- Cut 1: E, beige, position 9
- Cut 1: F, beige, position 10
- Cut 1: B, tan, position 3
- Cut 1: C, tan, position 4
- Cut 1: D, medium brown, position 7
- Cut 1: E, medium brown, position 8
- Cut 1: F, dark brown, position 11
- Cut 1: G, dark brown, position 12

For each of 12 Half Log Cabin blocks:
- Cut 1: A, blue, for the center
- Cut 1: B, tan, for position 1
- Cut 1: C, tan, for position 2
- Cut 1: D, medium brown, for position 3
- Cut 1: E, medium brown, for position 4
- Cut 1: F, dark brown, for position 5
- Cut 1: G, dark brown, for position 6

For the Center Star:
- Cut 4: 2 5/8" squares, muslin
- Cut 1: 4 1/4" square, muslin, cut again in quarters diagonally
- Cut 1: 7/8" x 20" strip, blue
- Cut 2: 7/8" x 20" strips, tan
- Cut 2: 5/8" x 7 3/4" strips, tan, for the star border
- Cut 2: 5/8" x 8" strips, tan, for the star border
- Cut 3: 7/8" x 20" strips, medium brown
- Cut 2: 7/8" x 20" strips, dark brown

In addition:
- Cut 2: 1 1/8" x 15 1/4" strips, tan, for the middle border
- Cut 2: 1 1/8" x 20" strips, tan, for the middle border
- Cut 2: 7/8" x 14 1/2" strips, blue, for the inner border
- Cut 2: 7/8" x 18 3/4" strips, blue, for the inner border
- Cut 2: 1 1/2" x 16 1/2" strips, dark brown, for the outer border
- Cut 2: 1 1/2" x 22" strips, dark brown, for the outer border
- Cut 2: 1 3/4" x 44" strips, dark brown, for the binding

DIRECTIONS
- Stitch 7/8" x 20" blue, tan, medium brown and dark brown strips right sides together along their length in that order, making a pieced panel. Stitch 7/8" x 20" tan, medium brown, dark brown, medium brown strips in that order making a second panel.
- Place the 45° line of your ruler along the edge of one fabric panel, as shown. Cut and discard the corner piece. Cut sixteen 7/8" strips measuring from this diagonal edge. Repeat, cutting sixteen 7/8" wide strips from the second panel. 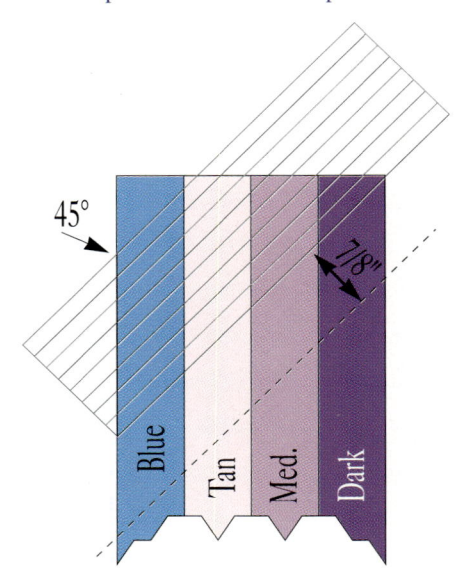
- Lay out 2 diagonal strips from each panel, exactly as shown. 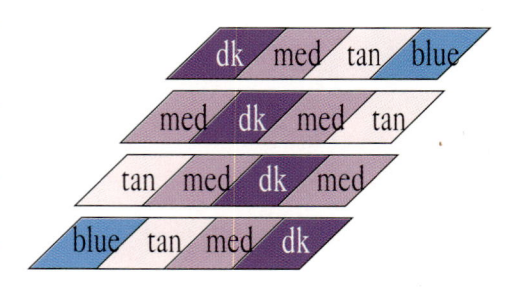
- Stitch the 4 strips together into a star point, carefully matching seams. Make 8 star points in this manner.
- Stitch the star points in pairs, sewing on the seamline only. Start and stop stitching 1/4" from the edges.
- Join pairs forming half the star. Sew

8

Mini Classics: Log Cabins

only on the seamline, as before. Join halves, in the same manner.
- Set the 2 5/8" muslin squares in each corner and the muslin triangles between the remaining star points.

- Square the star to 7 3/4".
- Stitch the 5/8" x 7 3/4" tan strips to opposite sides of the star.
- Stitch the 5/8" x 8" tan strips to the remaining sides of the star.
- Make 56 identical Log Cabin blocks by joining pattern pieces in order around the blue center square.

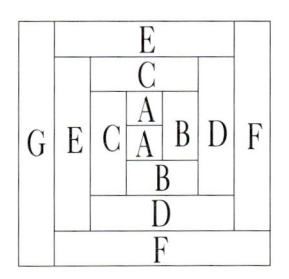

- Make 12 identical Half Log Cabin blocks in the same manner, noting the pieces are added to two adjacent sides of the center square. Allow the pieces to extend, as illustrated or trim them 1/4" from the sewing line.

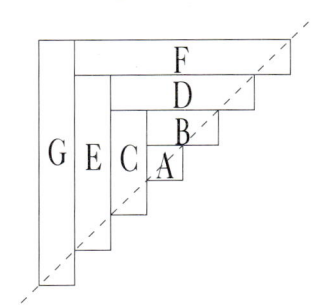

- Lay out 14 Log Cabin blocks and 3 Half Log Cabin blocks, as shown. Stitch

the blocks into rows. Join the rows to form 2 corner sections of the quilt. Make 2.

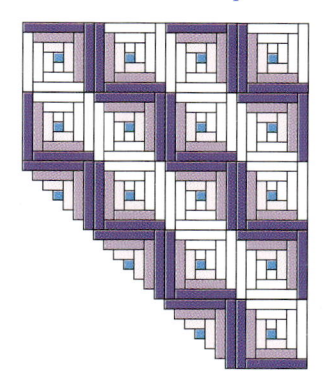

- Stitch a corner to opposite sides of the star block. Sew only on the seamline. Start and stop stitching 1/4" from the edges.

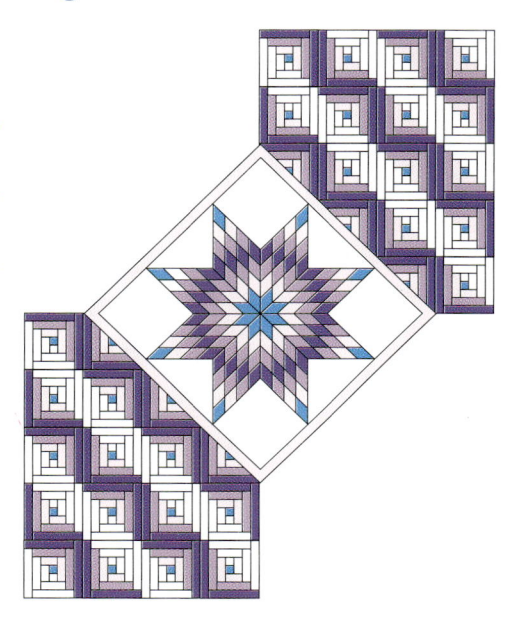

- Lay out 14 Log Cabin blocks and 3 Half Log Cabin blocks, as shown. Stitch the blocks into rows. Join the rows to form the 2 remaining corner sections. Make 2.

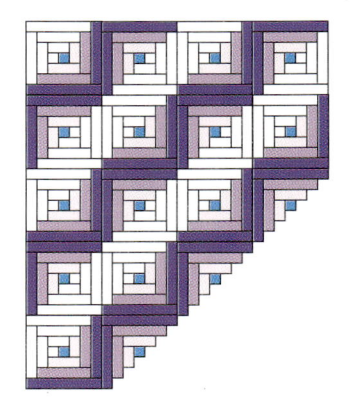

- Stitch the corner sections to the remaining sides of the quilt, sewing only on the seamline.
- Stitch the 4 open seams between the corner sections by folding the quilt in half right sides together, aligning raw edges. Stitch from the center out.

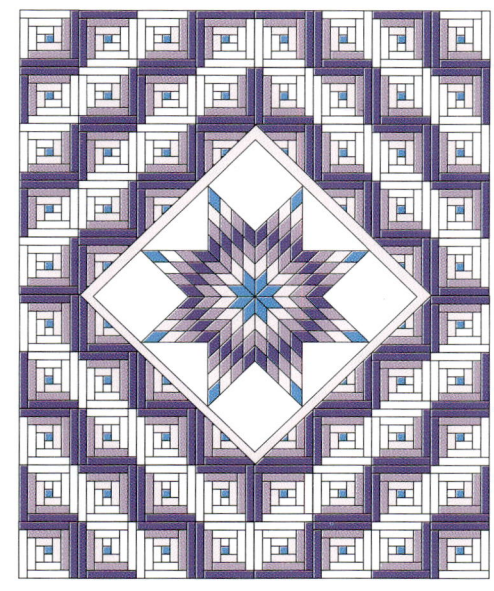

- Stitch the 7/8" x 14 1/2" blue strips to the short sides of the quilt.
- Stitch the 7/8" x 18 3/4" blue strips to the remaining sides of the quilt.
- Stitch the 1 1/8" x 15 1/4" tan strips to the short sides of the quilt.
- Stitch the 1 1/8" x 20" tan strips to the remaining sides.
- Stitch the 1 1/2" x 16 1/2" dark brown strips to the short sides of the quilt.
- Stitch the 1 1/2" x 22" dark brown strips to the remaining sides of the quilt.
- Finish as described in *Mini Stitching Tips*, using the 1 3/4" strips for the binding.

(Pattern Pieces continued on page 14)

Full-Size Block

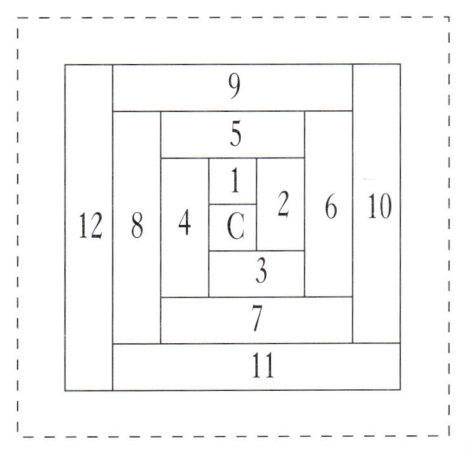

Mini Classics: Log Cabins

Use Eleanor Burns' strip-piecing method to make easy and accurate Log Cabin blocks for this *"Log Cabin Star"* (36" square) by Ruth Nies Gordy of El Cajon, California. Special thanks to Ruth for sharing her diagrams and notes! Pattern on page 2.

"Star in the Cabin" (18" x 21 1/4") was a hand quilted Mother's Day gift from JoAnn Stickler to her mother. The 56 tiny pieced Log Cabin blocks measure 1 3/4" square. Our version of this beautiful quilt has a center star 7 1/4" square, slightly larger than JoAnn's. The pattern is given on page 8.

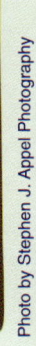

This quick and easy *"Half Log Cabin"* (16" square) is the perfect gift. The blocks can be set together in an endless variety and will be a constant source of pleasure. Our version was pieced on foundations by publisher Christiane Meunier, Montrose, Pennsylvania. The pattern is given on page 15.

10   Mini Classics: Log Cabins

Intermediate

Arlene Fleming of Cedar Falls, Iowa, stitched little 1 1/4" square Log Cabin blocks into *"Cabin Glow"* (5 1/8" x 6 1/2"). Arlene's inspiration for her mini was an antique wool Log Cabin quilt that was hand pieced by her husband's grandmother in the early 1900's. Arlene used a bright, fire-orange fabric to make the centers of her blocks glow.

Cabin Glow

Make this all-time favorite heart warmer!

QUILT SIZE 5 1/4" x 6 1/2"
BLOCK SIZE 1 1/4" square

MATERIALS
- Bright orange scrap for the Log Cabin block centers
- 2 light scraps and 2 dark scraps for the blocks and border
- 5 3/4" x 7" piece of backing fabric
- 5 3/4" x 7" piece of thin batting
- Paper, muslin or lightweight, non fusible interfacing for foundations

CUTTING
All dimensions include a 1/4" seam allowance.
- Cut 2: 3/4" x 5 1/2" strips, second dark scrap, for the inner border
- Cut 2: 3/4" x 4 3/4" strips, second dark scrap, for the inner border
- Cut 2: 1" x 4 3/4" strips, second light scrap, for the outer border
- Cut 2: 1" x 7" strips, second light scrap, for the outer border

DIRECTIONS
- Trace the full-size Log Cabin pattern (page 16) on your foundation material 12 times. Transfer all lines and numbers.
- Refer to *Mini Stitching Tips* for directions on foundation piecing. Stitch each of the Log Cabin blocks on foundations in numerical order. Use bright orange for section 1 of each block. To achieve proper color placement, use one dark scrap for sections 2 and 3. Use the second dark scrap for sections 6 and 7. Use one light scrap for sections 4 and 5 and the second light scrap for sections 8 and 9.
- Lay out the 12 Log Cabin blocks in 4 rows of 3 as shown in the Assembly Diagram. Refer to the photo as necessary for color placement.
- Stitch the blocks into rows and then join the rows. *Continued on page 16*

Assembly Diagram

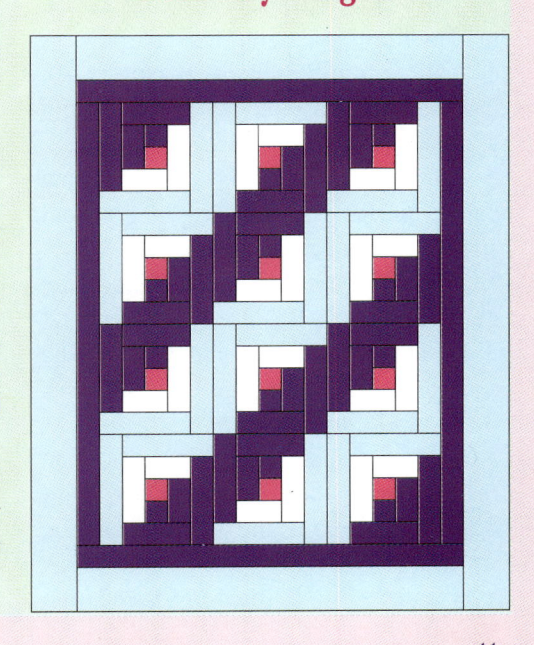

Mini Classics: Log Cabins

Intermediate

Shown on page 7

Corner Lot

Here is a fun way to use some of those scraps you've been saving— and foundation piecing makes it simple!

QUILT SIZE 17 5/8" square
LOG CABIN BLOCK SIZE 2 5/8" square
HOUSE BLOCK SIZE 5 1/4" square

MATERIALS
Yardage is estimated for 44" fabric.
- Several pieces of tracing paper, or piece of muslin or nonfusible interfacing at least 25" square
- Light and dark fabric scraps for the Log Cabin blocks and the house
- 3" x 7" piece of red, for the block centers
- 1/8 yard light-colored print, for the inner border
- 1/8 yard blue print, for the outer border
- 1/8 yard red print, for the binding
- 19 5/8" square of backing fabric
- 19 5/8" square of batting
- Glue stick

PREPARATION
- Cut 21: 5" squares, tracing paper, muslin or interfacing
- Cut 2: 3 1/2" squares, tracing paper, muslin or interfacing for the door and window units of the house
- Cut 2: 2 1/4" x 5 1/2" pieces tracing paper, muslin or interfacing for the roof and chimney units of the house
- Center a 5" square of your foundation material over the full-size Block Diagram. Trace all the lines and numbers on the square. Make 21, one for each block. This is the block foundation.
- Center a 3 1/2" square of foundation material over the Full-Size Door Unit. Trace all the lines and numbers on the square.
- Center a 3 1/2" square of foundation material over the Full-Size Window Unit. Trace all the lines and numbers on the square.
- Center a 2 1/4" x 5 1/2" piece of foundation material over the Full-Size Chimney Unit. Trace all the lines and numbers onto the material.
- Center a 2 1/4" x 5 1/2" piece of foundation material over the Full-Size Roof Unit. Trace all the lines and numbers onto the material.

CUTTING
Dimensions include a 1/4" seam allowance.
For the Log Cabin blocks:
- Cut 21: 1" squares, red print (log 1)
- Cut 21: 1" squares, light print (log 2)
- Cut 105: 1" x 2 3/4" rectangles, assorted light prints, for logs 3, 6, 7, 10 and 11
- Cut 63: 1" x 2" rectangles, assorted dark prints, for logs 4, 5 and 8
- Cut 63: 1" x 3 1/4" rectangles, assorted dark prints, for logs 9, 12 and 13

For the House block:
NOTE: *Individual measurements are not given for the pieces of the house. Just use scraps, making sure that the scrap is 1/4" larger than the section it is to cover on all sides.*
- Cut 1: 1 1/4" x 4 1/4" strip, green, for the grass
- Cut 2: 1 1/4" x 5 3/4" strips, dark print, for the borders of the house block
- Cut 2: 1 1/4" x 4 1/4" strips, dark print, for the border of the house block

Also:
- Cut 2: 1" x 13 5/8" strips, light print, for the inner border
- Cut 2: 1" x 14 5/8" strips, light print, for the inner border
- Cut 2: 2" x 14 5/8" strips, dark print, for the outer border
- Cut 2: 2" x 17 5/8" strips, dark print, for the outer border
- Cut 2: 1 3/4" x 44" strips, red print, for the binding

NOTE: *Sewing directions refer to the fabric (log) placement by number. Cross reference the cutting and sewing directions with the log numbers.*

DIRECTIONS
To stitch the Log Cabin blocks:
- For foundation piecing, the fabrics are always placed on the blank side of each foundation and stitched on the printed side. Refer to *Mini Stitching Tips* for detailed instructions on foundation piecing.
- Position and stitch logs around the block until you have added all 13 logs.
- Make 21 blocks in this manner.

To stitch the House block:
- Following the foundation piecing directions in *Mini Stitching Tips* piece the door, window, chimney and roof units.
- Make the individual units for the house, adding each piece of fabric in numerical order according to the numbers on the foundation, referring to the photo for color placement.
- Stitch the Door Unit to the Window Unit.
- Stitch the Chimney Unit to the Roof Unit.
- Complete the house by joining the top and bottom units together.
- Stitch the 1 1/4" x 4 1/4" green strip to the bottom of the house.
- Stitch the 1 1/4" x 4 1/4" dark print strips to the left and right sides of the house.
- Stitch the 1 1/4" x 5 3/4" dark print strips to the top and bottom of the house to complete the block.

FINISHING

- Lay out the Log Cabin blocks and the House block, referring to the Assembly Diagram. Stitch the blocks together into rows. Join the rows.
- Remove the paper foundations, being careful not to disturb the stitches.

NOTE: *If you used muslin or lightweight interfacing, the foundation will become a permanent part of the quilt.*

- Press lightly on the back.
- Stitch the 1" x 13 5/8" light strips to the sides of the quilt.
- Stitch the 1" x 14 5/8" light strips to the top and bottom of the quilt.
- Stitch the 2" x 14 5/8" dark strips to the sides of the quilt.
- Stitch the 2" x 17 5/8" dark strips to the top and bottom of the quilt.
- Finish according to *Mini Stitching Tips* using the 1 3/4" red print strips for the binding.

Full-Size Log Cabin Block

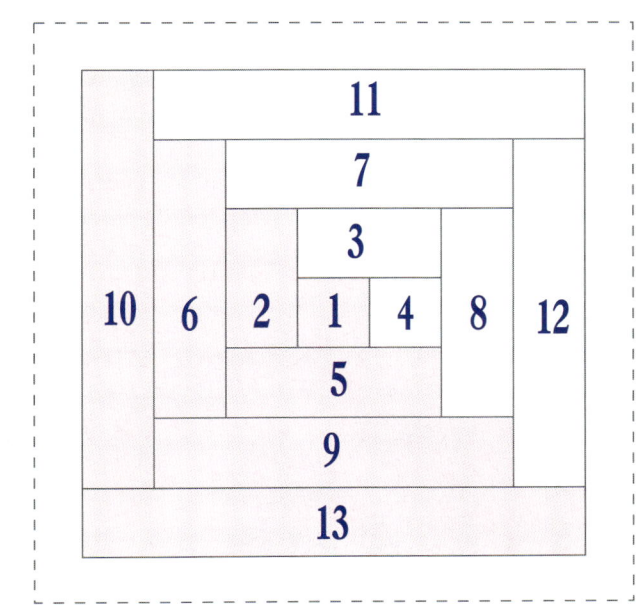

Full-Size Chimney Unit

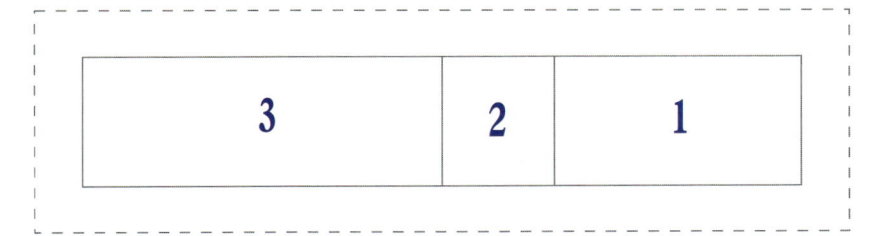

Full-Size Roof Unit

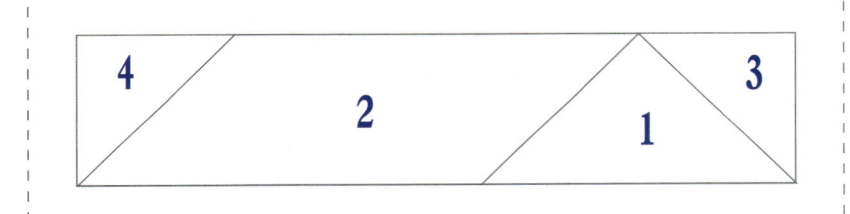

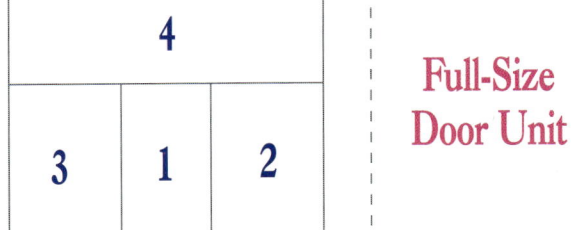

Full-Size Door Unit

Assembly Diagram

Full-Size Window Unit

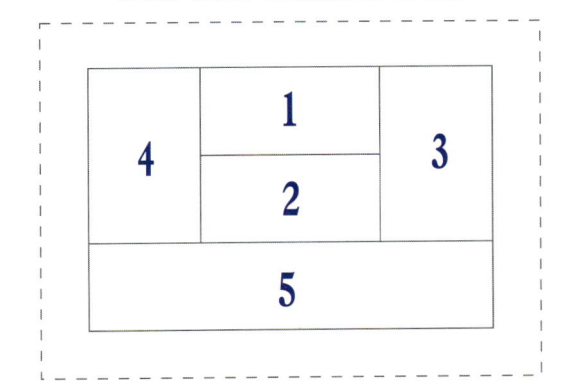

Mini Classics: Log Cabins

Easy
Shown on page 7

Log Cabin Barn Raising

Stitch yours on a firm foundation!

QUILT SIZE 7 1/2" x 10"
BLOCK SIZE 1 1/4" square

MATERIALS
Yardage is estimated for 44" fabric.
- Assorted dark scraps
- 1/8 yard white
- 1/8 yard print for the border and binding
- 9 1/2" x 12" piece of backing fabric
- 9 1/2" x 12" piece of thin batting
- Paper, muslin or lightweight, non fusible interfacing for foundations

CUTTING
Dimensions include a 1/4" seam allowance. The Log Cabin blocks are pieced on foundations. Use scraps that are 1/4" larger on all sides than the section on the foundation they are to cover.
- Cut 2: 1 1/2" x 8" strips, print, for the border
- Cut 2: 1 1/2" x 7 1/2" strips, print, for the border
- Cut 1: 1 3/4" x 44" strip, print, for the binding

DIRECTIONS
- Trace the full-size Log Cabin pattern on your foundation material 24 times. Transfer all lines and numbers.
- Refer to *Mini Stitching Tips* for instructions on foundation piecing. For each Log Cabin foundation, start with a dark scrap in position 1 and join fabrics in numerical order. Use white in positions 2, 3, 6 and 7. Use dark scraps in positions 4, 5, 8 and 9.
- Lay out the blocks in 6 rows of 4. Refer to the Assembly Diagram or photo as necessary to ensure that the dark sections of the blocks are placed properly. Stitch the blocks into rows. Join the rows.
- Stitch the 1 1/2" x 8" print strips to the long sides of the quilt top. Stitch the 1 1/2" x 7 1/2" print strips to the remaining sides of the quilt.
- Finish according to *Mini Stitching Tips*, using the 1 3/4" print strip for the binding.

Full-Size Pattern

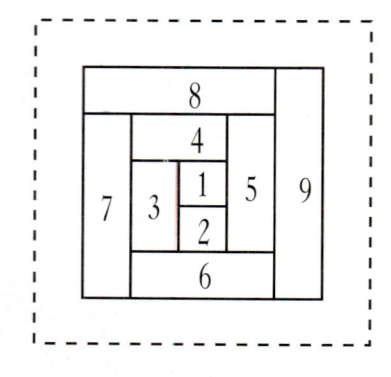

Assembly Diagram

Star in the Cabin Patterns
Continued from page 9

Full-Size Half Block

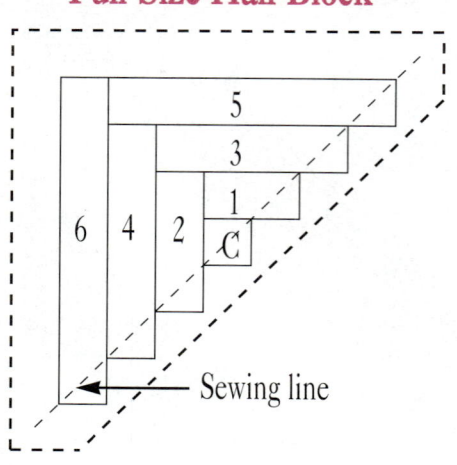

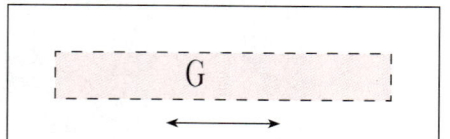

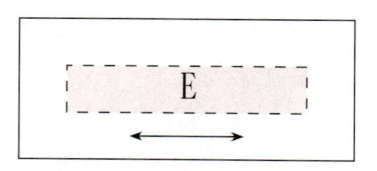

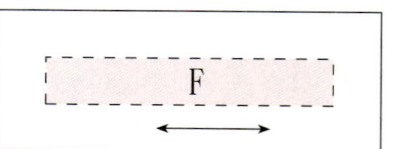

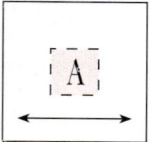

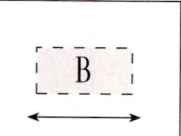

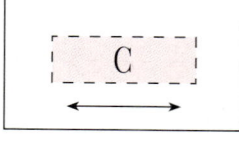

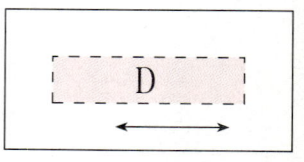

Sewing line

G

E   F

A   B   C   D

14   Mini Classics: Log Cabins

Half Log Cabin

You will want to make more than one!

QUILT SIZE 16" square
BLOCK SIZE 3" square

MATERIALS
Yardage is estimated for 44" fabric.
- 1/4 yard total of assorted light fabrics
- 1/4 yard total of assorted dark fabrics
- 12" x 18" piece of dark for the borders
- 9" square of red
- 18" square of muslin
- 18" square of backing fabric
- 18" square of thin batting
- Hot iron transfer pencil
- 4" square of tracing paper

PREPARATION
- Trace the full-size block on tracing paper using a hot iron transfer pencil. Transfer all the lines and numbers. Go over the lines again with the pencil.
- Following the manufacturers directions for the pencil, iron the paper pattern on the muslin 16 times leaving 1/4" between each block. Cut out the blocks 1/8" past the dashed line.

CUTTING
Dimensions include a 1/4" seam allowance. Cut 1" wide dark and light scraps for the blocks as you need them.
In addition:
- Cut 2: 2 1/2" x 12 1/2" strips, dark, for the border
- Cut 2: 2 1/2" x 16 1/2" strips, dark, for the border
- Cut 2: 1 3/4" x 44" strips, dark, for the binding
- Cut 16: 1 1/2" squares, red

DIRECTIONS
- Following the directions in *Mini Stitching Tips* for foundation piecing, complete 16 blocks. Use the 1 1/2" red squares in the center position. Use 1"-wide light strips in positions 1, 3, 5 and 7. Use 1"- wide dark strips in positions 2, 4, 6 and 8. Vary the fabrics for interest.
- Trim the blocks along the dashed line.
- Lay out the 16 blocks in 4 rows of 4, as shown, or in a pattern that you prefer.
- Stitch the blocks into rows. Join the rows.
- Stitch the 2 1/2" x 12 1/2" dark strips to opposite sides of the quilt.
- Stitch the 2 1/2" x 16 1/2" strips to the remaining sides of the quilt.
- Finish according to *Mini Stitching Tips*, using the 1 3/4" strips for the binding.

Easy
Shown on page 10

Full-Size Half Log Cabin Block

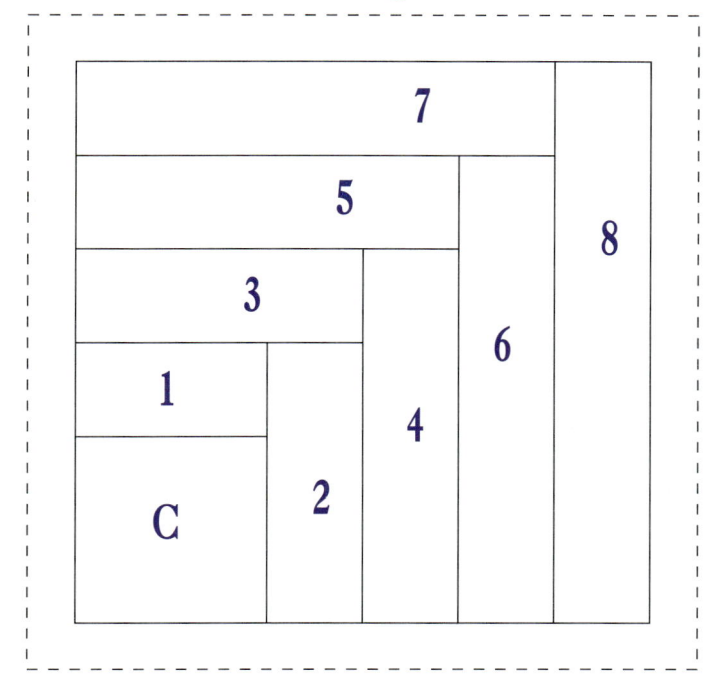

Assembly Diagram

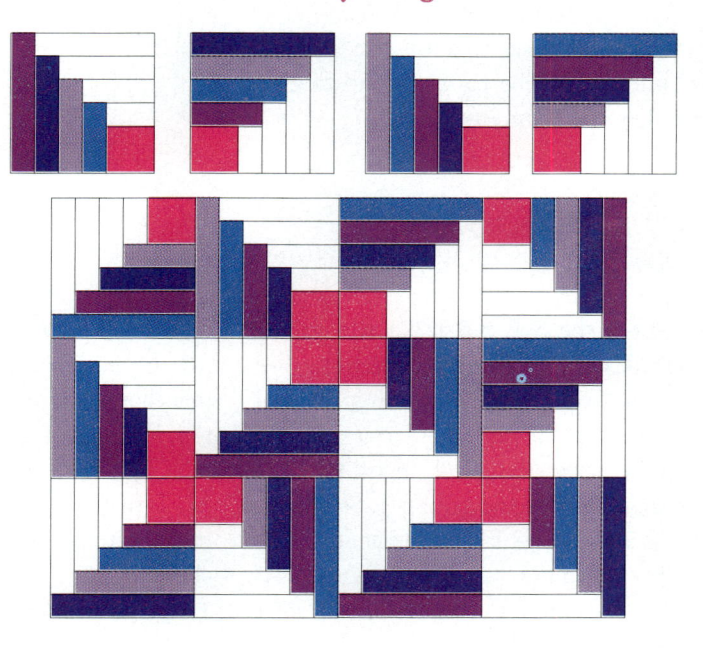

Mini Classics: Log Cabins

Challenging

Shown on page 6

by Joanne S. Nolt

Field and Furrows

This fun two-color mini will keep your hands busy!

QUILT SIZE 8 1/2" x 10 1/2"
BLOCK SIZE 2" square

MATERIALS
Yardage is estimated for 44" fabric.
- 1/8 yard tan
- 1/4 yard brown floral
- 10 1/2" x 12 1/2" piece of backing fabric
- 10 1/2" x 12 1/2" piece of batting
- Tracing paper for foundations

CUTTING
Dimensions include 1/4" seam allowance.
- Cut 4: 3/4" x 44" strips, tan
- Cut 4: 3/4" x 44" strips, brown floral
- Cut 4: 1 1/2" x 8 1/2" strips, brown floral, for the border
- Cut 1: 1 3/4" x 44" strip, brown floral, for the binding

DIRECTIONS
- For detailed instructions on sewing on foundations refer to *Mini Stitching Tips*.
- Carefully trace the full-size pattern 12 times on tracing paper, duplicating all the lines and numbers.
- Hand or machine stitch the 3/4" strips of tan and brown to the foundation, cutting lengths from the 44" strips as you need them. Use brown in positions 1, 2, 3, 6, 7, 10, 11 and use tan in positions 4, 5, 8, 9, 12 and 13.
- Complete 12 blocks.
- Lay out the blocks in 4 rows of 3. Stitch the blocks into rows. Join the rows.
- Stitch 1 1/2" x 8 1/2" brown strips to the long sides of the quilt. Stitch 1 1/2" x 8 1/2" brown strips to the remaining sides.
- Remove the paper foundation. I soaked my quilt in water until the paper dissolved.
- Press and finish according to *Mini Stitching Tips* using the 1 3/4" strip for the binding.

Full-Size Block for Field and Furrows

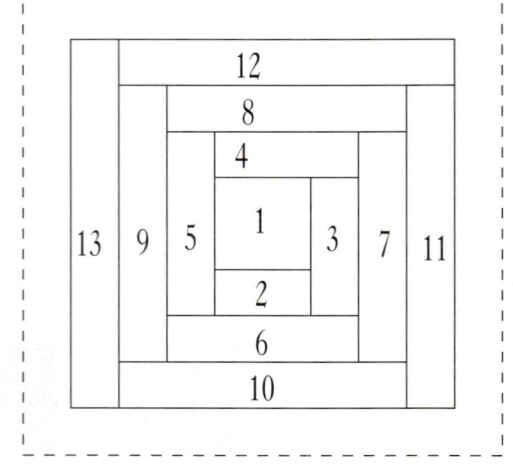

Assembly Diagram

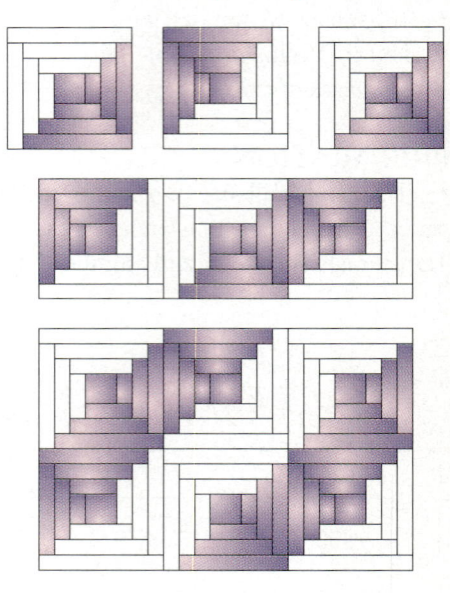

Cabin Glow

Continued from page 11

- Stitch the 3/4" x 5 1/2" strips to the long sides of the quilt top. Stitch the 3/4" x 4 3/4" strips to the remaining sides of the quilt top.
- Stitch the 1" x 4 3/4" light strips to the short sides of the quilt top. Stitch the 1" x 7" light strips to the remaining sides of the quilt top.
- Lay the quilt top right side up on a flat surface. Lay the backing fabric on the quilt top, right sides together. Lay the batting on the backing. Stitch the 3 layers together 1/4" from the edge of the quilt top, leaving a 4" opening for turning.
- Clip the corners to reduce bulk.
- Turn the quilt right side out through the opening and slipstitch the opening closed.
- Quilt as desired.

Full-Size Block for Cabin Glow

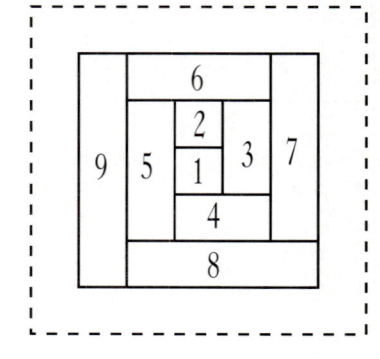